A Soul Beneath the Earth

A Holocaust Memoir of Faith and Resilience

Freda Perelmuter Schipper
with Sandy Schipper Wolberg

Copyright © 2022 by Sandy Schipper Wolberg
All Rights Reserved.

No part of this publication may be reproduced, stored in a retrieval system, or transmitted, in any form or by any means, electronic, mechanical, photocopying, recording, or otherwise, without the written permission of the author, except in the case of brief quotations embodied in critical articles and reviews.

ISBN 9798813947568 (paperback)
ISBN 9798829967888 (hardcover)

Printed in the United States of America

10 9 8 7 6 5 4 3 2 1

*Dedicated to
my children and grandchildren
with love and gratitude*

May the world never forget…

Table of Contents

Introduction i

Author's Preface ix

PART ONE: TESTIMONY

Chapter 1: From Darkness to Light 1

Chapter 2: A Brief History of Poland and the Rise of Hitler 3

Chapter 3: Family 7

Chapter 4: The War Comes to Horodlo 19

Chapter 5: The Beginning of the End 29

Chapter 6: The Uchanie Ghetto 43

Chapter 7: The Final Road (Dem Letstn Veg) 47

Chapter 8: The Selection 57

Chapter 9: Starzeń 63

Chapter 10: Escape 75

Chapter 11: Hiding 81

Chapter 12: Germany Retreats 91

Chapter 13: Hell Beneath the Earth 93

Chapter 14: Freedom 97

Chapter 15: A Sad Goodbye 105

Chapter 16: The Danger Continues 109

Chapter 17: Is This My Father? 123

Chapter 18: A New Life in Canada 133

Chapter 19: Mendel and Family.. 137

PART TWO: MEMORIES OF MY MOTHER

Chapter 20: Panic Strikes at EXPO 67 167

Chapter 21: My Yiddishe Mama.. 171

Chapter 22: The Trip to the Bank... 175

Chapter 23: The Phone Call.. 179

Chapter 24: A Magical Seder.. 183

Chapter 25: Liya... 187

Chapter 26: Dad... 191

In Memoriam 205

Legacy 207

APPENDICES

Appendix I: Freda's Poetry 213

Appendix II: Favorite Yiddish Idioms 219

Appendix III: The Budniewski Family 233

Appendix IV: Family Tree 235

Appendix V: My Surviving Family Members 247

Appendix VI: Yizkor 249

Acknowledgments 253

A Soul Beneath the Earth

Introduction

"It is impossible to adequately describe the horror of my 21-month confinement beneath the earth. Crouching in my pit and sharing my hideout with rats and vermin, I waited for the war to end. The days blurred into one another. I often thought to myself: Am I alive? Do I want to live?"

These are the words of my mother, Freda (Fradl) Perelmuter Schipper. They provide a snapshot of the horrors she survived during the Holocaust. Such experiences were beyond the comprehension of humanity when she was born to a distinguished religious Jewish family in Horodlo, Poland, on January 3, 1923.

She was 16 years old in 1939 when the Nazis invaded Poland. From 1939 to 1942 she worked in a forced labor camp and later watched in dread as the Nazis shoved her mother and siblings onto the train destined for Sobibor. On October 19, 1942, after escaping from a second labor camp, my mother arrived at the home of Katya and Matewka Budniewski, Ukrainian Catholics who had been friends of the family before and during the war. Matewka brought my mother food, clothing and shoes that helped her survive the backbreaking work in the labor camp. When she arrived at the Budniewskis' home, my mother learned that Matewka had built a small underground pit for her beneath a haystack in their barn. Remarkably, my mom remained in hiding there for nearly two years, keeping her sanity by writing poetry, crocheting, and teaching herself Russian.

The Budniewskis saved her life. Tragically, her family was not as fortunate. All the members of my mother's immediate family were killed, except her father, who miraculously survived a Siberian labor camp and was reunited with my mother after the war. Nearly 100 members of her extended family also perished.

My mother's unwavering faith in God kept her sane throughout impossible circumstances. What she viewed as a series of miracles enabled her to survive, while those around her were slaughtered.

A strong-willed woman with soft blue eyes, my mom constantly related her experiences with family, friends and even strangers. Speaking with conviction and determination, she set out to expose the Nazi's brutality and atrocities so people would know, and never forget, the death of six million of our people.

I often encouraged my mother to write a book about her experiences during the Holocaust, but she consistently demurred. Although she wanted her children to help her write her memoir, she did not want to burden them in any way. In truth, I think she did not want to do it until she felt her time to do so was running out.

On September 20, 2013, my mom was diagnosed with pancreatic cancer. Although we initially did not tell her the diagnosis, she was smart enough to figure out that her medical condition was grave.

After the diagnosis, my mother insisted she wanted to live at home by herself, stubbornly refusing help, remaining independent, and demonstrating the internal fortitude that kept her alive throughout the war. By that time, my father was already in a nursing home, his brain racked by Alzheimer's disease.

My mother knew the time had come to tell her story and she asked me to help her.

Introduction iii

I jumped at the chance. Competent, intelligent, and intuitive, my mom was my go-to person, my role model, and my friend. I knew she was pleased that I would work with her on the book.

We had to make a series of decisions: She lived in Montreal, and I lived in Woodmere, New York. How would we conduct interviews? Should I travel to Montreal? Should we speak over the phone? Should we record the interviews?

As always, my mom knew exactly how she wanted to proceed. She dictated the writing arrangements. We would conduct the interviews by phone. No tape recorder.

"I'll talk and you type it out," she instructed me.

For nearly three months, we spoke from 10pm to 1am almost every night except *Shabbos*, the Jewish Sabbath. During those three hours – while my 12-year-old son slept and my husband worked upstairs – I typed as quickly as I could, doing my best to capture her every word.

My mother wasted no time; she knew what she wanted to say. She spent the day preparing for our phone call by looking through her documents and writing out long-hand what she wanted to tell me, to make sure she did not leave anything out.

My mother insisted the manuscript be thorough, accurate, and reflect the harrowing truth of how the Nazis and the Poles persecuted the Jews during the war.

I imagined my mother writing her story by hand at the kitchen table. A self-taught scholar, my mother may have been looking for a reference in *Kehilat Horodlo*, the Horodlo *Yizkor* (Remembrance) book that she co-authored after the war, or browsing through books on Chassidim[1] to trace her family's history.

She relayed her story to me over the phone in great detail, drifting in and out of Yiddish as she traveled back to the time she worked at a labor camp, evaded Nazi capture, and hid in an

---

[1] Members of an Orthodox Jewish sect founded in Poland in the 18th century and characterized by its emphasis on mysticism, prayer, ritual observances, religious zeal, and joy.

underground pit. Sometimes she sounded calm, and at other times, overcome with emotion.

Some of the scenes she described were so horrific, her sorrow so deep and desperate, we would both cry.

But my mother checked herself. "We will continue working," she would say, regaining her composure.

After we got off the phone, I worked tirelessly to review what she told me and correct the grammar. At the start of the next call, she asked me to read what we wrote the previous evening. She knew she would not be around to edit the manuscript when it was done and wanted to hear how it sounded, to make sure it accurately reflected what she wanted to say.

Although I have been fortunate to share a close relationship with my mother, this project was an incredibly special gift to me as I prepared myself for her passing. I had always felt she would live forever and here she was at death's door.

I felt the closest to her when we worked on the book together. I thought about the hell she endured and felt proud that she was one of the few who lived to tell her story and honor the memories of the family members who perished.

During much of the time that we spoke, I knew my mother was in pain. With considerable resolve, she hid her pain and disability from everyone who knew her.

Our last interview took place on December 23, 2013. A week later, she was rushed to the hospital. We finished the manuscript just in time, as was God's will. I know, in my heart, that it gave her great comfort to share her entire story one last time with me before she passed.

This memoir is divided into two parts. In the first part, my mother describes her experiences during the war and provides a summary of her life after moving to Canada. In the second part, I offer a series of vignettes of some of my fondest and most profound memories of my mother's life and our relationship.

While in hiding, my mother wrote poems in Polish and Yiddish expressing her anguish, grievances, and prayers. English translations of her poems are included in Appendix 1.

My mother had a rich trove of Yiddish expressions that spoke to her character and wit. These Yiddish idioms can be found in Appendix 2. Appendix 3 gives an account of Matewka Budniewski and his family. Since her heritage was so important to her, I have included our family tree in Appendix 4. The final two appendices include an account of my mother's surviving family members and a *Yizkor* memorial, respectively.

There is a famous quote by Edmund Burke, an 18th century Irish statesman and philosopher: "The only thing necessary for the triumph of evil is for good men to do nothing." From 1933-1945, too many good men did nothing while bad men destroyed 12,000,000 souls, six million of them belonging to Jewish men, women, and children.

Whoever destroys a single life is considered by Scripture to have destroyed the whole world, and whoever saves a single life is considered to have saved the whole world.[2] This is a story of absolute evil in which the Nazis and their collaborators destroyed an entire world. It is also a tale of heroism in which one courageous Ukrainian farmer and his wife saved my mother's world.

It is with pleasure and privilege that I present to you my mother's memoir.

---

[2] Mishnah Sanhedrin 4:5; Yerushalmi Talmud 4:9, Babylonian Talmud Sanhedrin 37a

PART ONE
Testimony

Author's Preface

Rabbi Yochanan ben Zakkai's (circa 30 BCE - 90 CE) commentary about the inexhaustibility of Torah study[1] may well be adapted to describe the suffering of the Jewish people under the Nazis:

> *"If all the heavens were parchment, and all the trees pens, and all the oceans ink, they would not suffice to document all the torture and suffering of the Jewish people under the German occupation."*

Of course, the Germans did not act alone. Poles, Lithuanians, and Ukrainians also helped them kill Jews. Complicity was international: not one country in the world tried to intervene until they felt personally threatened; instead, they pretended to be unaware of the atrocities taking place. Even those few victims who managed to escape were refused sanctuary almost everywhere they fled.

I, Freda Perelmuter Schipper, witnessed the final journey that

---

[1] The following quote is attributed to Rabbi Yochanan ben Zakkai: "If all the heavens were parchment, and all the trees pens, and all the oceans ink, they would not suffice to write down the wisdom that I have learned from my masters."

the Jewish people of Horodlo, Poland, were forced to take to the crematoria in Sobibor. It began eight days after *Pesach* (Passover) in 1942, when the Horodlo Jews were expelled to the Uchanie ghetto, and ended on June 10, 1942,[2] when all the Jews from the Uchanie ghetto were forced onto the trains in Miaczyn that were headed for the Sobibor death camp. Like millions of other Jews, the members of my beloved family died in great agony. Many survived years of terrible suffering only to be murdered at the very end of the war. Meanwhile our murderers went on to live full lives, some continuing to enjoy the possessions they stole from their victims. Few were ever punished.

Sixty-eight years have passed since the end of the war, but time can never erase my pain or the images of evil that have haunted me throughout my life. They are as vivid in my mind as if they happened yesterday. The pale faces hollow with hunger, backs bloodied from whippings, bodies crippled from torture, the walking dead – these never disappear. There are no words to describe the horrors that I witnessed. Those lucky enough to have lived a life free of such atrocity can never comprehend the viciousness that we experienced at the hands of the Germans, Poles, Ukrainians, and Lithuanians.

As for me, the terror of not knowing what the day will bring has remained with me forever. So, despite the pain it causes me to remember, I must record these things so the rest of the world will never forget.

Freda Perelmuter Schipper
Montreal
2013

---

[2] *Kaf hay Sivan tav shin bet* in the Jewish calendar.

CHAPTER ONE

From Darkness to Light

I was unable to speak, stand or see the sky for nearly two years. Like a terrified mole, I hid from the Nazis and their collaborators in a pit dug beneath a haystack in a barn owned by my Ukrainian savior. When I emerged on July 24, 1944, I did not have the strength to stand. I was like a newborn fawn struggling to find its feet but could not. I had to be carried like a baby in the arms of the man who risked his life for mine. My first breath of fresh air in nearly two years felt like being revived from the dead. Taking in the placid scene around me I wept. It was the first day of my second life. I was just 21 years old.

At the time, I had no idea what date or time it was. The Nazis were gone, and I was free. I had thought my savior and his family had fled with the evacuation of Horodlo, as the war front was moving closer to our town. I thought I was alone, but this righteous gentile never left. He too hid from the Nazis in an underground pit. When he came to take me from what could have easily been my grave, I was still unsure I was safe. I did not know if I would ever be safe in a world that had gone mad.

Before going into the pit, I knew that my oldest brother, Moshe Levi Yitzchak, had been murdered. My father had attempted to cross the Bug River to the Ukraine, was captured by the Soviets and sent to a labor camp. I had seen the Germans load my mother and my three younger siblings onto the cattle cars, presumably headed for the Sobibor death camp. I prayed that I would live so that I might one day be reunited with my family. When I finally emerged from my underground haven, I felt guilty that I was still alive. I had little hope that my mother, two younger brothers and sister survived. Nevertheless, I prayed every day that I would see them again, *but how would I ever find them? And my father, was he living? Did he somehow make it through these last six years of hell?*

The Jews of Poland, and most of Europe, were gone, exterminated like worthless pests. It was not the first or only genocide of the 20th century, but the Holocaust was unlike any that came before or since. Jews were murdered for the crime of existing and the Final Solution was meant to kill every Jewish man, woman, and child.

Millions of Jews had been reduced to ashes, blown from the chimneys of Auschwitz, Sobibor, Majdanek, Belzec, Treblinka and Chelmno. Friends, family, and neighbors were humiliated, tortured, gassed, and shot. Their families might never learn their fate and could never mourn at their graves because so many had been cast off like garbage into pits. In the span of six years, 90% of Polish Jewry, and almost two-thirds of all European Jewry were annihilated.

CHAPTER TWO

A Brief History of Poland and the Rise of Hitler

On the eve of World War II, Poland had the highest concentration of Jews in Europe, 3.5 million, comprising 10 percent of the country's population. You might think this was because of the benevolent treatment Jews received from the Poles, but you would be wrong.

Jews were encouraged to come to Poland by medieval princes who hoped the Jews would help modernize the economy. The Jews became moneylenders because of the Church's prohibition against usury. Since they were banned from owning land, they became merchants, artisans, and professionals. The Jews prospered, provoking jealousy and anger among competitors and peasants who interacted with them. Later, the otherness of the Jews was exacerbated by their failure to assimilate. Dominated by Orthodox traditions, the Jews dressed differently than their compatriots and primarily spoke Yiddish rather than Polish.

The situation for Jews grew worse after Poland's acceptance of Christianity in the tenth century, leading to centuries of persecution. As in other places and times, the refusal of Jews to accept the new religion set them apart and made them targets of antisemites. Jews were viewed as Christ killers and accused of the ritual killing of Christians, what is now referred to as a blood libel. Jews purportedly used the blood of Christians to make *matzoh* (a thin, unleavened bread) for the Passover holiday. Jews were burned at the stake and subjected to massacres because of these beliefs.

Although the Holocaust is unique in its horrific magnitude and vicious approach to murder, and although there has never been a time when so many Jews were murdered as in the six years of World War II, the Nazis would not be the first invaders to murder Jews in Poland. That distinction belonged to the Cossack Bogdan Chmielnicki. In 1648, the Cossacks instigated an uprising against the Jews when Chmielnicki convinced the Poles that they were sold as slaves to the "accursed Jews." Many Jews fled the country, but approximately 100,000 were murdered, and nearly 300 Jewish communities were destroyed. Between 1648 and 1651, Jews in Poland experienced the kind of horrors that would later befall their descendants under Hitler. In the city of Mogila, for example, the Cossacks murdered 700 Jews. There were widespread accounts of women and children thrown into graves and buried alive. Jews were ordered to kill each other, and women were tortured and raped. Elsewhere, the invaders slaughtered Jews with butcher knives and destroyed the synagogues. Torah scrolls were thrown in the street for men and animals to trample.

After being broken apart by its neighbors in the 18th century, Poland ceased to be an independent state by 1795. Poland did not reemerge as a sovereign nation until the end of World War I. Newfound independence did not correspond with increased tolerance, however, as Jews came under attack on the pretext that they were communist spies. Even after signing the 1919 Versailles Minority Treaty, which was meant to protect the rights of minorities, Jews were threatened, in part to demonstrate the Poles' objection to external interference in their internal affairs.

After Germany adopted the Nuremburg Laws and other discriminatory measures taken by the Nazis against the Jews, the Poles implemented their own restrictions. Jews were barred from employment in state-owned monopolies, civil service jobs, and even were limited to working at textile mills owned by Jews. Boycotts of Jewish businesses were enforced by antisemites preventing customers from entering Jewish establishments. Jews who attended universities faced discrimination and threats as well. Those schools that accepted Jews would not allow them to sit with the other students and Jews were often attacked by their classmates.

There were many pogroms that occurred across Poland before the outbreak of World War II. In 1936, for example, a pogrom occurred in Prztyk, which one historian described as the most notorious incident of antisemitic violence in Poland in the interwar period.

In that same year, the Polish Foreign Minister, Józef Beck, told the Polish parliament that the country only had room for half a million Jews. This meant the remaining three million would have to find new homes. How would such a mass deportation take place and where would the Jews be sent? He demanded that the League of Nations make provisions for the annual departure of between 80,000 and 100,000 Jews from Poland. A commission subsequently investigated the possibility of Jewish migration to Madagascar, which was considered a suitable site for the resettlement of European Jewry, in part because it was so far from Europe. The idea was dropped two years later when it was determined the island could accommodate only a few thousand people. The Nazis revived the idea in 1940, but it was overtaken by events. The invasion of Europe was going to bring even more Jews under Nazi control and the number was too great to consider shipping them off to the island.

Although no one could have foreseen the horrors to come, many Polish Jews were scared enough to seek a way out of the country. Unfortunately, even before the war started, countries around the world were shutting their doors to immigrants. The British had largely sealed off Palestine in response to Arab complaints and violence. Even the United States tightened its quotas in the 1930s, accepting fewer than 7,000 immigrants – Jews and non-Jews – annually from Poland. The attitude of most countries toward Jews and other immigrants was summed up by an unidentified immigration official who was asked in 1939 how many Jews would be allowed in Canada after the war. He replied, "None is too many."

My family decided to stay in our home in Horodlo. The consequences of that decision would prove catastrophic.

CHAPTER THREE

Family

I was born on January 15, 1923[1] and raised in the small Polish town of Horodlo in Hrubieszów County, Lublin Voivodeship in eastern Poland. Horodlo is on the west side of the tree-lined banks of the Bug River bordering Polesie and Volhynia close to the border with Ukraine. The town was established around 1287; Jews are first mentioned in this area in 1507 and were granted citizenship in 1565. In roughly 1628, the first synagogue was built.

---

[1] Sandy's note: Throughout her life, our family celebrated my mother's date of birth as January 15, 1925. It took many years for my mother to confess that her year of birth was, in truth, 1923. Despite our curiosity, she never disclosed the reason for the two-year disparity to me or my brothers.

My mother was actually born on the 15th day of the Hebrew month of Tevet ("*chatzi* Tevet" or half the month of Tevet) in the Hebrew year 5683. In preparing her tombstone, my brothers and I were surprised to discover that she never knew the true day of her birth. With the help of the internet, we discovered that the Julian date corresponding to the 15th of Tevet, 5683 is in fact January 3, 1923.

I would like to make the following conjecture. Growing up in an Orthodox Jewish family in Poland, the Hebrew date, and not the Julian calendar equivalent, was the date she celebrated her birthday. I am inclined to think that when a Julian date was required of her, she converted the 15th of Tevet to the 15th of January, the month of January roughly corresponding to the Hebrew month of Tevet. This would explain why much of Freda's documentation, during and after the war, states her birthday as January 15, 1925.

The town was invaded and destroyed by foreign armies and invaders many times. As recently as 1850, the entire wooden town burned to the ground, including the synagogue, which was rebuilt out of brick in 1865. Gradually, the town grew, and Jews comprised one-third of the general population of 2,112 by the end of the 19th century. By 1934, there were about 1,000 Jews in Horodlo.

If anything, my life was comfortably predictable. I would help at home with chores and assist in the care of my younger siblings. It was expected that I would go to school until an appropriate *shidduch*, or match, was made for me. I would marry, bear and raise children, and most likely remain within a stone's throw of my parents' home for the rest of my life. I would have given anything for that life when I crawled out from under the barn a half decade later.

We were five children, three sons and two daughters, and we lived comfortable lives. My mother, Chaya Petil Zawidowicz Perelmuter, was a loving homemaker typical of the times in which we lived. My father, Nosson Nuta Perelmuter, owned a grocery store and sold bottles of soda he brought from his father's soda factory in Chelm, where he grew up.

Education was a priority for my parents. During the day, we went to school with the gentile children; after school, I attended a private Hebrew school and my brothers went to *cheder*, a traditional Jewish elementary school that taught Hebrew and Talmudic studies.

We lived strictly Orthodox religious lives and were highly respected in our community because of our relation to several well-known, prestigious, rabbinical dynasties. My maternal great grandfather, Rabbi Yekutiel Gelernter, a descendant of 39 generations of rabbis dating back to King David, served as the rabbi of Horodlo in the second half of the 18th century. His legacy continued with his son-in-law, Rabbi Moshe Yehuda Leib Halevi Berman, who succeeded him as the rabbi of Horodlo during my lifetime.

Rabbi Gelernter's wife, Fradl, my namesake, was the granddaughter of Rabbi Pinchas Shapira of Koretz (1726-1791), a leading Chassidic figure and *Talmid Chaver* (colleague) of the Baal Shem

Family 9

Tov, who was the founder of Chassidic Judaism.

My family's rabbinical dynasty extends to Rabbi Gershon Henoch Leiner,[2] the third Rebbe of Izhbitze-Radzin. He was married to one of Rabbi Gelernter's sisters, Hadassah.

Growing up, my parents, four siblings and I lived with my maternal *bubbe* (grandmother), Ziesl (Zysl, Zysla, Ziesele) Gelernter Zawidowicz and one of my mother's sisters, Chana, her husband Moshe Tennenbaum, and their three children, Leibale, Ziskind, and Fradale. We all lived together in the house that we inherited from my great grandfather, Rabbi Yekutiel Gelernter. My *zeide* (grandfather), Aryeh Leib Zawidowicz,[3] Bubbe Ziesl's husband, made a comfortable living by assessing forests for their building materials and lumber for a firm in Warsaw. Sadly, Zeide Aryeh Leib died in 1924, leaving Bubbe Ziesl to raise their eight children on her own.[4] Although I was an infant at the time of his death, I grew up hearing many wonderful stories about my grandfather.

My *bubbe* Ziesl was smart and educated. She raised eight children and learned remedies to heal the sick. Before the war, it was not uncommon for someone who was ill or giving birth to request Bubbe Ziesl to their bedside. If someone could not afford a doctor,

---

[2] Rabbi Gershon Henoch Leiner was known for his pioneering efforts to reintroduce the *mitzvah* (religious commandment) of *techeiles*, which was lost to the people of Israel for 2,000 years. *Techeiles* represents the fringes of the *tzitzis* that were dyed a royal blue using the extracted secretion from a *chilazon* mollusk. He was the author of many Chasidic *seforim* (books) including the *Orchos Chaim, Sod Y'sharim, Tiferes Hachanochi,* and *Dalsos Shaar Ha'ir*. He is referred to as the *Orchos Chaim* based on his seminal book by the same name. See "The Radziner Relation" in the family tree, Appendix IV, page 238.

[3] Aryeh Leib Zawidowicz's sister, Chaitshul Zawidowicz, was married to Rabbi Avraham Yehoshua Heshel Leiner, the brother of Rabbi Gershon Henoch Leiner. They were the matchmakers of my parents. In the summertime, I often visited my paternal grandparents in Chelm, and spent time at Chaitshul's house. As a little girl, I remember the attention lavished upon me by their nephew Mordechai Yosef Elazar Leiner, who would later assume the title of Radziner Rebbe.

[4] See family tree entitled "Bubbe Ziesl and Zeide Leibel's Eight Children and their Families." Appendix IV, pages 239-242.

Bubbe Ziesl was summoned. She was held in such high regard that on *Yom Kippur*, the holiest day of the year, people would line up in front of her house to obtain a blessing from her.

Bubbe Ziesl was one of my favorite people and I have always tried to emulate her greatness. She was 83 years old when she was brutally murdered by the Nazis.

Our small Orthodox community was isolated from the world, so we had no idea what was happening to the Jews just beyond the Polish border in Germany.

Hitler had come to power in 1933, but we were not aware of the Nuremberg Laws and the various other ways the Nazis were persecuting the Jews. It was not until November 9-10, 1938, that we learned of the serious danger to Jews in Germany and Austria. During those 24 hours, which came to be known as *Kristallnacht* (the Night of Broken Glass), thousands of Jewish men were rounded up and sent to a new prison – not yet known as a concentration camp – called Dachau. During the night and early evening, Nazis and their sympathizers roamed the streets throughout Germany and parts of Austria, burning synagogues and their holy books and scrolls, shattering the windows of Jewish-owned stores and looting them, beating and humiliating Jews, and stealing their possessions. By the end of the night of terror, at least 96 Jews in Germany and Austria were murdered, 1,300 synagogues and 7,500 businesses were destroyed, and countless Jewish cemeteries and schools were vandalized. Approximately 30,000 Jews were imprisoned.

In retrospect, this was the beginning of the Holocaust. From that point on it should have been clear that the fate of Jews under the Nazis was precarious. Immediately following these horrible events, Jews still had an opportunity to escape; in fact, they were encouraged to leave. Most, however, did not want to leave the only homes they had ever known. They refused to believe, even after the preceding years of persecution, that they would not be treated and protected as the loyal German citizens they were.

The events in Germany were disturbing but remained a problem only for Jews in Germany and Austria. The lack of response to *Kristallnacht* by the world, however, emboldened Hitler. The unwillingness to act against Germany, or to defend the Jews, reinforced Hitler's belief that Jews were non-humans who were expendable, and that he could pursue his genocidal agenda with impunity. In January 1939, he gave a speech promising the destruction of the Jewish race in Europe. The world did not take his words seriously.

Little did we know that less than ten months later we would find ourselves in the shoes of our Jewish brothers and sisters in Germany.

Freda Perelmuter, at age sixteen, with her family, not long before the war. Left to right (top row): Freda; Freda's mother, Chaya Petil (in the background); Freda's eldest brother, Moshe Levi Yitzchak, age eighteen. Left to right (bottom row): Freda's brother, Yekutiel, age eight; her sister, Bracha Tsirel, age four; and her brother, Mordechai Yosef Elazar, age ten. Horodlo, 1939.

Freda's father, Nosson Nuta Perelmuter. Horodlo, 1939.

Freda's mother, Chaya Petil Zawidowicz Perelmuter. Horodlo, circa 1940.

Zu der am Dienstag den 19 März d. j. 1918 in Horoldo, Stattfinden der Hochzeitsfeier der Herrn
N. Perelmuter
mit Fräulein
Ch. Zawidowicz
beehren sich hiermit höflichst, einzuladen.
die ELTERN und das BRAUTPAAR
Trauung um 8 Uhr Abends.

Wedding invitation of Freda's parents. Poland, 1918.

Freda's eldest brother, Moshe Levi Yitzchak. Horodlo, 1937.

Freda's maternal uncles, Yekutiel Zawidowicz (left) and Mordechai (Mottel) Zawidowicz (right).

Freda's maternal grandparents, Aryeh Leib (Leibel) Zawidowicz and Ziesl Gelernter Zawidowicz.

Left to right (rear): Three of Freda's five maternal uncles, Yosef, Fishel, and Yekutiel Zawidowicz. Seated left to right (front): Yosef's wife, Ruchel Boksenboim Zawidowicz and Freda's grandmother, Ziesl Zawidowicz. Standing left to right (front): Yosef and Ruchel's children, Fradl (Chedva) and Yankel Zawidowicz.

Freda's aunt and maternal uncle, Malke and Mordechai (Mottel) Zawidowicz.

Freda's first cousins, Surale (standing) and Chanale (seated on sled), the daughters of Malke and Mordechai Zawidowicz.

Freda's uncle, Moshe Tennenbaum, the husband of Chana Zawidowicz, Freda's maternal aunt.

Two of Freda's first cousins who shared the same Yiddish name, Fradl: Fradl Tennenbaum, the daughter of Chana Zawidowicz and Moshe Tennenbaum, and Fradl Zawidowicz, the daughter of Fishel Zawidowicz.

Freda's maternal aunt, Malke Zawidowicz, and her husband, Avner Zucker.

Freda's great aunt (Zeide Leibel Zawidowicz's sister), Chaya (Chaitshul) Zawidowicz Leiner, 1937. Freda's mother bore a striking resemblance to her great aunt.

*Boating on the Bug River.
First person on left: Freda's first cousin, Yosef Chaim Zawidowicz.*

Family 17

Center: Freda's paternal aunt, Esther Perelmuter. Chelm, 1929.

Freda's paternal uncle, Leibish Perelmuter.

Freda's paternal aunts, Malka Perelmuter, seated center, and Dina Perelmuter, standing on the right. Chelm, 1939.

CHAPTER FOUR

The War Comes to Horodlo

*I*n the week leading up to the invasion of Poland, the Germans and the Soviets signed the Molotov-Ribbentrop pact, an agreement not to attack each other. A secret part of their plan was to divide Poland between them. The original dividing line was supposed to be the Vistula River. However, on September 1, 1939, the Germans invaded Poland and a few weeks later the two governments agreed to move the border east, making the Bug River the boundary between German-occupied Poland and the Soviet Union.

By September 26, the Nazis occupied Horodlo and life as we knew it ended. At the time, my oldest brother, Moshe Levi Yitzchak, was eighteen years old and, at sixteen, I was the second oldest. My younger brother Mordechai Yosef Elazar was ten, my brother, Yekutiel, was eight, and my little sister, Bracha Tsirel, was only four.

When the Nazis took over, they issued special documents identifying us as Jews and we were required to wear a Star of David sewn either onto our clothes or on an armband. This was only the first step in the Nazis' plan, but at that moment we could not have imagined what was to come.

Having our country overrun and then experiencing a flurry of discriminatory measures directed at Jews was like a whirlwind.

Many Poles were willing Nazi collaborators against the Jews. The Nazis cultivated these antisemites and fascists and, together, they conducted pogroms around the country. The opportunity to attack Jews and loot their stores and homes proved an incentive for more Poles to join the Nazi attacks.

News of Nazi atrocities outside our small world managed to filter through to us despite all the restrictions we faced about listening to the radio or reading papers. We knew that on December 1, 1939, the German SS rounded up all the Jewish males between the ages of sixteen and sixty in Chelm and forced them to march to the town of Hrubieszów, about thirty miles away. They also seized all the Jewish men and boys in the small towns and villages along the way and concluded the abductions with those in Hrubieszów itself. From there, they forced roughly 2,000 prisoners on a grueling death march. Not far outside Hrubieszów, the SS shot about twenty-five people in cold blood, supposedly because they had mounted a rebellion. In fact, it was a warning to the others not to resist or try to escape. The march continued for days.

We did not even know the term "death march" then, nor did we know that these events were only a foreshadowing of the horrors to come. Many of those who had been taken were shot along the way because they could not keep up with the murderous pace set by their well-armed SS guards. Anyone who stumbled and fell was immediately killed. At some point along the way, the group was divided in two. Half were marched to the river bordering Soviet territory in Sokal and ordered to swim across. A few survived. None of the other group who were forced to march to Belzec was as "fortunate." The few who arrived alive after their sixty-mile march from Chelm were shot, their bodies thrown into the ditches on the side of the road.

My father's cousin, Moshe Szulman, was among them. His murder was the first of almost a hundred in my family.

The terrible news of what had happened to the Jews of Chelm and Hrubieszów caused immediate panic in Horodlo. Certain that the men and boys in our community would suffer the same fate, many searched for ways to flee across the Bug River to the Soviet side. Desperate to escape the Nazis, my father managed to find a Polish peasant who, for money, was willing to row him across the river to Volodymyr-Volynsky.[1] My mother's two sisters, Malke Zawidowicz Zucker and Chana Zawidowicz Tennenbaum, were living there with their husbands Avner and Moshe and their families. Bubbe Ziesl and my oldest brother, Moshe Levi Yitzchak, had joined them, along with my aunt, Pearl Biderman Zawidowicz and her family – three of her four sons, her daughter-in-law, and her two-year-old granddaughter. They all prayed that they would be safe there. All anyone could think about after September 1939 was where to find safety.

Other Jewish men and boys from Horodlo and the nearby towns and villages were not as lucky as my father. Many of them were robbed and then drowned by the very Poles they paid to row them across the river; their supposed saviors made off not only with their fees, but also with their Jewish passengers' meager possessions. As if this were not horrible enough, some of the Jews who tried to swim to safety were shot in the water by German soldiers. Our river began to bleed red from dead Jews. The gruesome image of our once-serene river filled with floating corpses is seared into my memory.

Although my father's crossing was uneventful, Volodymyr did not prove to be a haven for him. Like most of the Polish Jews who succeeded in escaping the clutches of the Nazis, my father fell straight into the waiting arms of the Red Army. Instead of being allowed to remain peacefully with his family, my father was immediately sent to a labor camp in northern Siberia. I would not see or hear from my father for nearly five years.

Day by day, the prospect of escape for any of us dwindled. At around the same time, Polish and Ukrainian mobs revolted against

---

[1] This city is known by several names: Wlodzimierz-Wolynski (Polish), Volodymyr-Volynsky (Ukrainian), Vladimir Volynsky (Russian), and Ludmer (Yiddish).

the Jewish population. They stripped anything and everything from the Horodlo synagogue, leaving behind only the building structure – four windowless walls and the roof. They also dismantled the wooden fences that surrounded the Jewish homes. The Jewish cemetery was destroyed – the fence was disassembled and taken away, tombstones were smashed, and graves desecrated. As if this were not enough, the skulls of the Jewish deceased were hoisted on sticks and paraded in front of Jewish homes.

It is hard to describe our bitter life under the German occupation. By 1941, nearly all Polish Jews were isolated in some of the worst areas of towns and villages and confined to ghettos. Starvation, illness and executions in these ghettos took the lives of thousands of men, women, and children. Our town only had 125 Jewish families. It was so small that the Germans did not need barbed wire to confine us and so we remained in our homes. Food was becoming scarcer. We ran out of wood, so we used our floors, stairs, and whatever we could find, to burn for warmth and cooking.

As time passed, the Nazis slowly began to empty the ghettos. The Jews who were deported had no idea they were being transported to their death. As each ghetto was closed, more penniless Jews were herded into the remaining ones where many were reduced to begging. We endured hunger, cold, torture, disease and humiliation from the Germans and the Poles as well. We lived in constant fear, never knowing what new misery the day would bring. The Germans issued new edicts every day.

The Nazis established a *Judenrat*, a Jewish Council, to implement their orders. Many of their decisions made the difference between life and death. For example, all Jews had to wear white armbands with yellow Stars of David on them. A curfew was imposed, forbidding Jews from being outside after 7 p.m. Jews were prohibited from leaving the Jewish district and were banned from walking to the gentile parts of town. Death was the punishment for anyone violating these orders.

The *Judenrat* became very controversial after the war. Some people argued they should not have helped the Nazis, even if it meant their execution, because they had no right to condemn other Jews to death. Others defended the *Judenrat* by noting that they had little choice to keep their families alive. Moreover, if they refused to cooperate, the Nazis would have found others to take their place. The members of the *Judenrat* carried a heavy burden, which only became weightier with each new order from the Nazis. After the war, I learned that the head of the Warsaw Ghetto *Judenrat*, Adam Czerniakow, was ordered to choose 10,000 Jews each day for deportation. The strain and the shame led Czerniakow to commit suicide. The head of our *Judenrat*, Pesachye Blat, was an extremely pious and learned Jewish man who was murdered when he attempted to persuade the Gestapo to call off the deportations of the Horodlo Jews.

In the early spring of 1941, the Germans were preparing to breach the Molotov-Ribbentrop pact and invade the Soviet Union. They needed to pave the muddy roads of Horodlo so they could move their cars and tanks through the town. They enlisted Polish bricklayers to demolish what was left of the synagogue, the Jewish cemetery, and all the Jewish stores, to provide bricks and tombstones to pave the roads. The Germans later used the cemetery as a pasture.

One of the *Judenrat's* responsibilities was to organize work groups for slave labor assignments. I was assigned to gather bricks and load them onto wagons. Starting at the top of the buildings, the Polish bricklayers would take apart the bricks and throw them down onto the street where the Jews helplessly stood. We then lifted the heavy stones and hoisted them onto wagons. The debris from the falling bricks fell into our eyes and blinded us; our hands were cut from lifting the broken stones. The Germans stood by with whips and those who did not work fast enough were lashed. The Polish bricklayers turned the work into a cruel game as they tried to hit the Jewish laborers below with the bricks, while Polish "policemen" were quick to brandish their whips when a Jew hesitated. Whenever a Jewish target was struck, the bricklayers, the police, and their Nazi overseers erupted in cheer. One of the Polish policemen had lived and worked in my town before the war. He had been my neighbor.

Our work party could go home for lunch and, on that first day, I returned home in extremely poor condition. I was exhausted and my eyes were full of painful splinters. I tried to rinse out my eyes and wanted to return to work, but, seeing my suffering, my brother Yosele, who was twelve at that time, volunteered to take my place so I would have a chance to rest. I returned to work about an hour later and, as I drew closer, I saw people looking at me hesitantly, fear and worry in their eyes. I felt a growing sense of trepidation that something bad had happened. When I arrived, I saw Yosele with his back covered in blood that had soaked through his shirt. Our neighbor, the Polish policeman, had whipped him so ferociously that the skin on his little back had split. Despite his condition, he continued to work, knowing that to stop would mean more torture.

Without worrying about the consequences, I grabbed Yosele and left. Crying all the way, I took my brother to the house where the policeman lived. When the policeman's wife opened the door, I lifted Yosele's shirt and showed her the lacerations on his back, telling her that her husband had whipped him. Knowing that their only son was the same age as my brother, I shouted: "How would you feel if someone did this to your son?" She was so startled that she could not answer. Then I turned and left. When Yosele and I got home, my mother and I took care of him, doing whatever we could to ease his pain.

The next day, I returned to work. Now the task was to pave the road with the stones we had gathered.

***

On June 22, 1941, the Germans crossed the Bug River in Operation *Barbarossa*, the invasion of the Soviet Union. As I mentioned earlier, part of our family, including my aunt Malke, her husband Avner, and their son and daughter, Leibel and Fradale, were living on the Soviet side of the river in Volodymyr. When the Germans arrived, they immediately imposed a curfew. Unaware of the rules,

Malke's six-year-old daughter, Fradale, ran outside after curfew hours to play in her yard. Malke immediately went to bring her back into the house, but she was not quick enough. Both mother and daughter were still outside when a German officer passed in front of the house. The rest of the family was nervously waiting inside the house when they heard a shot followed by silence. They were terrified, too afraid to go outside and see what had happened.

Early the next morning, after spending a long, anxious night, they ran outside into the yard. At first, they did not see anybody. The yard appeared to be completely empty. Then they noticed one area of the yard where the earth appeared to be disturbed, as if someone had been digging there. When they began removing the top layer of soft earth, they found the bodies of Malke and Fradale. Malke was shot in the foot and her little daughter was holding her tightly around the waist. She had no bullet wounds. Both mother and daughter had been buried alive. This was the first *korban* (blood sacrifice) in the town of Volodymyr.

Beginning on July 5, 1941, the Germans carried out numerous mass executions in the Volodymyr prison courtyard. On September 30, 1941, *Erev Yom Kippur*, the eve of the Day of Atonement, the holiest day of the Jewish calendar, they ordered two hundred young men to slave labor detail. In a field near the jail, these men were tortured and forced to dig the grave in which they would then be buried. My brother, Moshe Levi Yitzchak Perelmuter, age twenty, was among those murdered. We heard stories of how the ground shook because many of the victims were buried alive.

It did not take long for the devastating news of my brother's murder to reach me and my family in Horodlo. I have a clear recollection of the disturbing exuberance in which the tragic news was delivered to us by our Polish neighbors. Worse still, is the image I carry with me all these years of the grief-stricken face of my mother and her inconsolable sobbing when she learned that her eldest child had been killed. Life in Horodlo after the German occupation was horrific, but at that time, nothing could have seemed worse than the death of my brother.

The mass executions of Jews continued in Volodymyr throughout the fall and winter of 1941. On April 13, 1942, the Jews were forced into a ghetto. This was one of several established around Poland with the aim of forcing as many Jews as possible into a confined area. The Lodz ghetto had a population, for example, of 160,000 Jews in 1940, the Warsaw ghetto, nearly half a million.

Life in the ghetto was tenuous. On September 1, 1942, the Germans launched a major *Aktion* (an operation involving the mass assembly, deportation, and/or murder of Jews) in Volodymyr. Four thousand Jews were murdered in the prison courtyard and buried in mass graves. With their Ukrainian collaborators, the Germans besieged the town so that no Jews could escape. They went from building to building and chased all the adult Jews out into the streets and loaded them onto trucks. The infants and children were flung from the windows directly onto the trucks, which were then driven to the Piatydni area, twelve kilometers west of Volodymyr. When they arrived, 14,000 Jews were machine-gunned by the infamous *Einsatzgruppen* – the Nazi mobile killing squads comprised of both German and Ukrainians soldiers – and buried in pits. My aunt Pearl, Aunt Chana and her family, and Aunt Malke's husband and son were among the dead.

Freda's brother, Moshe Levi Yitzchak. Volodymyr, 1940.

By the time this terrible event was over, on September 3, 1942, approximately 4,000 Jews remained in the ghetto. Among them were my aunt Ruchel Boksenboim Zawidowicz and Chaya Zisberg, a niece of Pearl Zawidowicz. Ironically, although most of the

Jews tried to hide from the Germans, my *bubbe* Ziesl remained in her house, and clutching her *siddur* (prayer book) she continuously prayed. She was not caught at that time.

On November 13, 1942, however, the Germans began another *Aktion* and the remaining members of my family were all caught and slaughtered in the field near the Volodymyr jail where my brother had been murdered. A few years later, I met a girl who had survived this final *Aktion* in Volodymyr. She told me that my *bubbe* Ziesl had recited the *Viddui* (confessional prayers for atonement) for the end of life with the remaining Jews just before their deaths. She only had one question for God at that time: *Why did He let her live to witness the deaths of all her children and so many of her grandchildren?*

By the end of December 1942, the vast majority of the Jewish community of Volodymyr was gone.

Throughout 1942, the Nazis deported Jews to concentration camps. In Horodlo, we had heard rumors of men, women and children being taken away to parts unknown, sometimes in the middle of the night. We had come to know that Jews who were confined to ghettos were forbidden to leave, and Poles were warned against helping the Jews. Death was the punishment for anyone disobeying these orders. Although the Nazis were executing people for attempting to escape, this did not stop many Jews from trying to flee or some Christians from aiding them.

CHAPTER FIVE

The Beginning of the End

*W*itnessing the fate of so many of my family members and friends filled me with so much fear and dread, but it also strengthened my resolve to fight to survive.

From 1939 until 1942, I worked with other Jewish men and women in a forced labor brigade in the German *Kommandantur*, the German headquarters, not far from our house in Horodlo. We did not get paid or receive any food. I took it upon myself to work when I was chosen and to substitute for my mother, fearing that she may not survive the Germans' brutality. At that time, the soldiers patrolled the perimeter of the fields and ensured that the Jews obeyed orders. Although they were not Gestapo, the soldiers were nonetheless ruthless. Throughout the town, Jews were beaten, tortured, and humiliated by these "soldiers." Houses were looted. The contents of stores were emptied into the streets and Poles ran to grab whatever they could get their hands on.

Those of us who worked in the *Kommandantur* were given special documents indicating that we were employed there so we could not be sent to work elsewhere. There were many gardens and fields around the German headquarters and our job was to tend to these fields. One soldier, a professional gardener, supervised us. The work was extremely difficult as we spent long hours in the hot sun with no food.

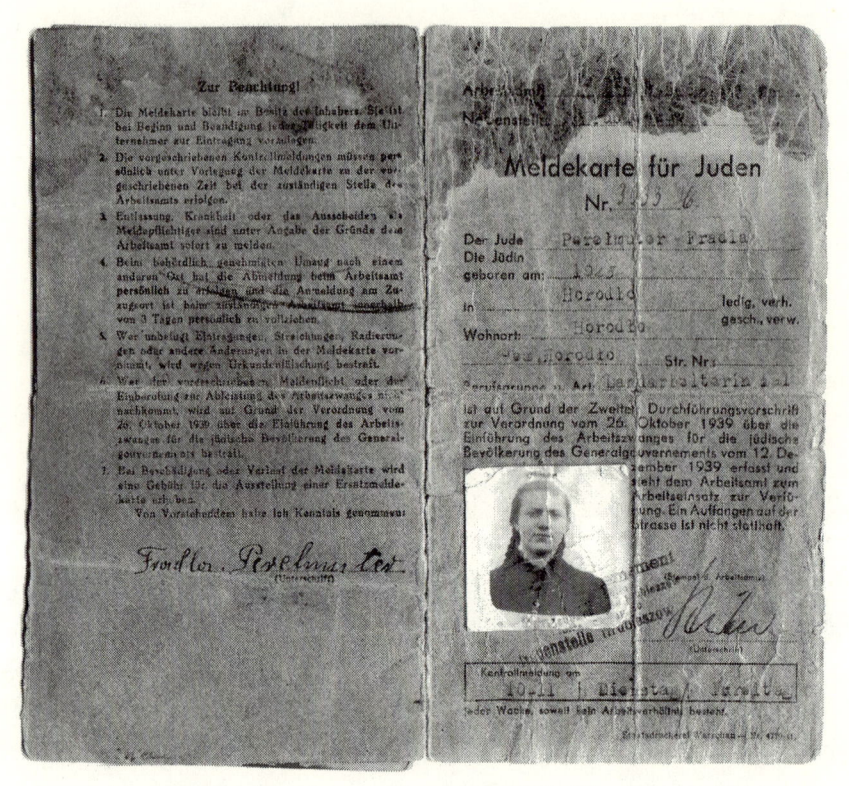

The work identification card issued to Freda in Horodlo in 1939.

From time to time, officers would select girls to clean their living quarters. This was a far better job because it got us out of the hot sun. I was so adept at cleaning, that one officer always selected me for this assignment. I scraped the floors, cleaned the toilets, and made sure to polish all the doorknobs. When I found his boots, I polished them too. He was so pleased with my performance that he made sure I stayed behind to work for him when my labor detail was first ordered out of town. This kept my family and me together for a little bit longer. On a few occasions, he would give me a piece of bread, which I saved for later and shared with my siblings.

When food became scarce, we had no choice but to sneak out to the gentile areas of town to exchange whatever items we had left in the house. I volunteered to be the one to go since I feared that my mother would be caught; there could be no worse outcome than losing her. I took a gold tooth, a silver spoon, cooking utensils, and any possession I could trade for some flour and potatoes.

Making these exchanges was extremely hazardous and difficult. I would sneak outside into the cool hours of darkness, right before curfew time. The gentile neighborhood was far from where we lived. I ran most of the way, trying to stay hidden. There were times that my barter brought me as much as twenty-five kilograms of potatoes. The load was so heavy I was forced to crawl home on my hands and knees with the sack perched on my back.

In addition to running out of food, we did not have any wood to cook and heat our house. We broke up all the wooden objects we had in the house – the chairs, the floors, and the steps – and used the wood to cook our meager food. We could not use our fences from around our yards because they had already been dismantled and stolen by the Poles.

To make matters worse – and it was hard to believe they could get worse – there was an outbreak of typhus in our town. The Germans went house-to-house searching for the sick. Jews who were found to have typhus were taken away, and instead of bringing them to a hospital, as the Germans promised, they were taken outside the town and shot.

In some houses, entire families were so sick with typhus that they were unable to care for one another. My mother was so determined to help the sick that she learned how to apply *bunkes* (heated glass cups used for the therapy now called Fire Cupping) to promote healing. Whenever she did not see a family in the streets, she would visit and try to help; bringing with her some food such as soup made of water and mashed potatoes from our own inadequate supplies.

One day, my mother went to a neighbor's house to find everyone there sick with typhus. A three-year-old girl named Surale Brenner was covered in red spots and feverish, and her parents were too ill to help her. It was the middle of the winter and there was no heat in their house. My mother covered Surale with her apron and carried her under her shawl to our house. She wrapped the child in a warm blanket and placed her near our oven to keep her warm. I was terrified! I knew how contagious typhus was and I worried that we would all get sick. I argued, "Don't you know you're bringing disease into our house?" My mother said that she was certain that our family could not escape the typhus epidemic and was determined to assist this one child. She could not let her die, she told me. She prayed, bartering with God, that in the merit of caring for this child, her family would not all get sick at once. My mother's prayers were answered. We did contract typhus, but we got sick one at a time.

During the time that I was flushed with fever, at the height of my typhus illness, a neighbor's daughter warned us that the Germans were going door to door searching for the sick. To this day, I cannot imagine the source of my mother's strength. I was completely helpless. She lifted me out of bed, quickly dressed me, and propped me up on a bench with my back supported by the oven. She applied some rouge to my pale face to give my cheeks some color, covered my thinning hair with a kerchief, and put a book on my lap. I was so sick and feverish, my vision blurred, and I could not see the letters on the page. When two German soldiers came into our house, they saw that the beds were made, and the house was in order. They then turned to me and asked if I was enjoying my reading. I was so frightened I could hardly breathe. My heart raced and fear parched my mouth. Miraculously, they left without waiting for an answer. I am not sure I could have given them one. That night I went through terrible sweats and my fever broke. Although I recovered, it took a while before my vision returned and my hair grew back.

In this hellish environment, we still made all attempts to observe our Jewish customs and rituals. My brother, Mordechai Yosef Elazar (Yosele), was to become a *Bar Mitzvah* just before *Pesach* (Passover) in 1942. One of our very learned neighbors, Rabbi Shmuel Zisberg, undertook the task of preparing him. Every day, Yosele went to Rabbi Shmuel's house to learn his *parsha* (Torah portion) while the rabbi's wife, Rebbetzin Blima, stood guard at the window. If she saw a German soldier approaching the house, she would signal his arrival by stamping her feet on the floor. Yosele would then run into an armoire, which opened at the back to an outside door that led into their backyard. From there he would make his way back to our house.

We managed to secure a pair of *tefillin*[1] from a woman whose husband had been killed. The *tefillin* were old and large. Regardless of their size and age, my brother was thrilled to receive them. He was so proud to reach the age of thirteen, to come of age.

Even in these tragic times, Jews still *davened*, or prayed, in secrecy. When Yosele was called to complete the *minyan*, a quorum of ten men over the age of 13 required for public worship, he could not have been more excited. He would come back to our house and exclaim, "*Momme*, can you imagine that they waited for *me* for a minyan?!"

***

In the beginning of 1942, we began to hear rumors that the Gestapo was rounding up Jews from their towns and cities and relocating them to places unknown. These people disappeared without a trace. We also learned that the Germans were sending Jews to concentration camps.

Fear gripped the Jews of Horodlo, and a disquieting silence settled on our *shtetl* (village). We all recognized that horrible events were coming our way. We prepared rucksacks to be ready for our exile. We stopped undressing before going to sleep, worried that the Germans would raid our houses during the night. Alarmed and unnerved by these unfathomable reports of torture and death, we entered *Pesach* of 1942.

That spring, we observed *Pesach* in our house and Yosele led the *Seder* (a ritual service and dinner for the first two nights of Passover) with my youngest brother, Yekutiel. We shuttered our windows and covered them from the inside with bedspreads so that the dim lights

---

[1] *Tefillin* is a pair of black boxes with leather straps that contain Hebrew parchment scrolls. Jewish men don these phylacteries for weekday morning prayers.

we used for reading could not be seen. Our *Seder* meal consisted of a few dry potatoes and a few *matzohs* that we had baked in secrecy in someone else's house. The observance of the Passover *Seder* with the reading of the *Haggadah* is quite long and Yekutiel dozed off several times. Each time, Yosele would threaten that if Yekutiel did not stay up to complete the *Seder* with him, he would report Yekutiel to our father when he returned home. I always think about how much they missed my father and how much we hoped that one day we would be reunited.

Approximately eight days after *Pesach*, our turn for deportation came with the arrival of the Gestapo to our town. The Jews of Horodlo were given two days to gather their belongings and assemble in the marketplace for transport. There were a few exceptions. Anyone who was working in the fields for the German headquarters had to remain and Jews who worked for Polish farmers could also stay. Some Jews paid farmers to employ them so they would not be transported. I received a document from the *Kommandantur* stating that I was needed to work in the fields. I knew that those who were transported away never returned but I had no idea what happened to them. I hoped that I could somehow find where the rest of my family was being taken and help them.

Safeguarded for many years after the war by the sister of Matewka, Freda's savior, this floral porcelain bowl was used in Freda's home in Horodlo for the potatoes served on the Passover holiday. It was delivered to Freda by a friend who visited Matewka's sister in the Ukraine.

The leader of the *Judenrat*, Pesachye Blat, decided to collect what little valuables the Jews had left to persuade the Gestapo to call off the transports. He and another Jewish man traveled to Hrubieszów to arrange this deal with the Gestapo. The Germans took their package filled with valuables, followed them as they left, and killed them both. That day was a *chorban* (destruction) in our little *shtetl*. When people learned of the murders, panic set in. People were crying, screaming, and fainting. We all gathered in the house of Sarah Mindel Rosenbloom to say *Tehillim*, prayers from the Book of Psalms. We realized that we were all doomed.

During the two days prior to our evacuation, the Jews of Horodlo attempted to sell off all their remaining possessions. Cognizant of our predicament, our Polish neighbors squeezed us to sell at low prices. I knew that our friends, a farmer by the name of Matvey (Matewka) Budniewski, and his wife, Yekaterina (Katya), were interested in buying our beautiful armoire. I ran to their house and told them to come and get it. Matewka disassembled it and took it home piece by piece. He had wanted our two matching beds as well, but unfortunately, by this time, the mayor of our town – who was of German descent – had confiscated the rest of our furniture, as he had done to many other Jews in our town. Matewka offered to give us 1,000 zlotys for our armoire, which was the full price we had paid. He did not want to take advantage of our desperate situation. Since he did not have all the money available, he gave us a down payment and promised to give us the rest at a future date. At that same time, my mother asked him for a few loaves of bread, but he did not have any to give us. It was during the sale of this armoire, that my relationship began with the Budniewskis.

I divided the money from the armoire among my mother and my siblings, sewing pockets inside the linings of their jackets and hiding it there. I did not take any of the money for myself. I wanted so much to protect them. We managed to bring many of our household goods such as coats, clothing, bed sheets, and bedspreads, to some of the Christian people in our town for safekeeping. After the war, our Christian "friends" refused to return these items to us.

There was a Polish woman in our town named Wladka who made her living before the war lighting the stoves for Jews on *Shabbos*. While she was going from house to house, Wladka would leave her daughter, Lodzia, at my *bubbe* Ziesl's home. My mother became friendly with Lodzia and they stayed friends even after they both married. Lodzia's husband, Mr. Grabarcsuk, sold firewood and, during the war, my mother gave Lodzia some of my father's clothes in exchange for this vital firewood that we so desperately needed to cook our food. Lodzia took the clothing but never delivered the wood. She did not want to have any contact with us Jews.

On the morning of our transport, Lodzia unexpectedly came to see us. We thought she had come to say goodbye, perhaps to even bring us something to take on the road. Instead, to our surprise, she asked my mother to give her my only coat, the coat I was wearing. She wanted the coat for her daughter and told my mother that since we were all going to be murdered, it was better that she would have it rather than the Germans. My mother became so enraged that she screamed at her, "My daughter will outlive your daughter!" and evicted her from our house. Many years after the war, I learned that Lodzia's husband, son and daughter had all died young. Lodzia survived and was confined to a wheelchair.

* * *

Although I was ordered to remain in Horodlo to continue working for the Germans, I accompanied my mother and siblings to the marketplace. As we left our house, my mother turned back to give it a last look. "God knows," she said, "if I will ever see my home again." I too, looked back at our beautiful home and garden – a quick glance at the blossoming trees that had been planted by my eldest brother. My heart was broken.

Forever embedded in my memory is the image of the evacuation of the Jews from Horodlo – the despondency and anguish seen on the faces of the men, women, and children as they were leaving their houses. Witnessing the speed at which our Polish neighbors moved into our houses and took over our possessions was astonishing, inconceivable, and painful.

We arrived at the marketplace to find most of Horodlo's Jews gathered there, and Poles in their wagons happily waiting to drive us out of "their" town.

We hugged, kissed, and cried as my mother and siblings were herded onto the wagons. I watched them as they waited until orders were given for the wagons to move. Suddenly, to our surprise, I saw in the distance our Ukrainian friend, Katya Budniewska running toward us with a sack on her back. This angel had brought us eight loaves of hot bread that she had baked during the night.

I watched my mother, my two brothers and my little sister being driven away in one of the wagons, thinking that I would never see them again. I had no idea that the Germans were transferring the Jews to the nearby town of Uchanie before deporting them to the Sobibor death camp.

Wailing and shrieking, and without concern that the Gestapo would notice me, I made my way home. Adding to my despair, I was utterly shocked to return to my house and find that it had already been taken over by a Polish family. I told the woman that all I needed was my knapsack, but she refused to give it to me. I was furious and threatened to complain to the *Kommandantur*. Upon hearing that, she grabbed my knapsack from the house and threw it out onto the road.

There were almost no Jews left in town – only those who were working for the Poles or Germans. No one could return to their houses because, on the same day that the Jews were deported from Horodlo, the Poles confiscated the Jewish homes and moved in. All the workers assigned to the *Kommandantur* were given one house to live in; this house became our new "home."

***

A day after the transports out of Horodlo, I arrived at the *Kommandantur* expecting to continue my work in the fields. The *Kommandant*, however, picked a group of about eight of us and assigned us to clean up a school that had been repurposed as horse stables, and make it livable for the Gestapo. I boldly asked the

Kommandant why I had been selected for this task. I told him that I was very worried that I may never return, since making any mistake while working for the Gestapo could be punishable by death. He answered that he had to pick the best workers and I was among them. He also said that he had demanded a guarantee from the Gestapo that we would all return. *Could I believe the "guarantee"?*

Cleaning up the stables was a disgusting task. The stench was indescribable. There was so much manure and filth on the wooden floors that we stood paralyzed, not knowing where to begin. Under the watchful eye of a German soldier, I took charge and assigned jobs to each worker. First, we had to remove the manure from the floors, cleaning one small part at a time. I organized our team so that the boys who were with us were responsible for bringing water from the well. Two of us would wet the floor, two others would scrub the floor with hand brushes, some would then rinse the floor and make sure everything was spotless, and then others would wipe it dry. We repeated this process in each room. By day's end our job was done, and we prepared ourselves to return to the communal house.

As everyone was leaving, I was ordered by the German soldier to return the next day to help their cook. I was terrified to go by myself. Knowing that water needed to be carried from the well for cooking, I suggested that one of the boys come with me. The boy's name was Yitzchak Feigenbaum, the son of Mordechai Feigenbaum, our *shochet* (a ritual slaughterer needed to prepare kosher meat).

The next day, when everyone else returned to the *Kommandantur*, Yitzchak and I went to the stable that had been converted into the Gestapo quarters. We were both wearing our patches with the Star of David, but as soon as we arrived, I took off my sweater so the Gestapo would not know I was Jewish. I did not look Jewish – I had blue eyes and blond hair that I wore in two long braids, so I blended in with non-Jews who also worked there.

My assignment was to peel hundreds of potatoes as Yitzchak brought water from the well to wash them. The cook warned me that each potato skin had to be peeled very thinly so as not to waste

Freda's friends, cleaning the stables for the Germans. Feeling so humiliated, Freda refused to be in the photo.

any part of the potato. In addition, the potatoes had to be carefully examined for blemishes. I had to work fast. When I finished peeling the potatoes, I was told to cut up the onions, spices, and other ingredients the cook needed to make a roast. The roast was huge – it had to be enough to feed about fifty Gestapo officers. I would not have been able to lift the pot; luckily, the cook agreed to do that. As I stood in a foyer cutting onions, I saw the cook struggling to light the fire in the stove, so I went over and offered to light it for him. He watched in amazement as I placed a piece of firewood horizontally on the fire, laid the other pieces on top, then took a small sliver of wood, dipped it in kerosene, and put it under the wood that I had placed horizontally. I lit a match to the sliver of wood and lit the stove. He was incredibly pleased.

When the Gestapo officers arrived for their lunch, they sat in the dining area drinking and singing as they waited for their food. The cook decided that I would be the one to serve them their trays of food. I was horrified! Working behind the scenes was frightening enough, but interacting with the Gestapo was spine-chilling. As I began to serve the inebriated men their food, the leader asked:

"Are you Polish?"

"No," I answered.

"Are you Ukrainian?"

Again, I answered no.

"So, what are you?" he asked me.

I started trembling and quietly said, "I am a *Jude*" (a Jew).

The chief of the Gestapo burst into laughter and then he asked if my mother was Jewish.

"Yes," I said.

"And your father?"

"Yes," I answered sheepishly.

Then he loudly exclaimed, "Well, your mother could have been Jewish, but you never really know who your father was!"

They all laughed.

I lived.

When I finished serving, I returned to the provisional foyer and sat with Yitzchak. To our surprise, the cook came out of the kitchen carrying two plates full of meat and potatoes for us. Yitzchak quickly gulped down his portion and when I offered him my plate, he gladly finished it too. As hungry as I was, I could not bring myself to eat the non-kosher meat. Taking notice of this, and admiring me for adhering to my religious convictions even in these terrible times, the cook brought me enough bread and jam that I had some left over for dinner.

I worked with this cook for eight days, going back to the communal house at night and returning in the mornings. As I was returning home one night, Bracha Blat, the daughter of Pesachye Blat, came running toward me crying. She told me that the Gestapo had arrested her mother, Ruchel, and two other men named Avraham Zajdel and Moshe Berger. The three had been thrown in jail. She begged me to go back to the Gestapo and ask for their release. I turned back to honor her request; fortunately, the Gestapo officers were no longer there. If I had spoken to them, I am certain that I would have been thrown in jail with the others. I made my way home and Bracha joined us since the rest of her family was gone.

Living in a house close to the prison, we were able to watch through the windows and see what would happen. Around midnight, we witnessed two Gestapo men open the jail door and escort their captives out. We had no idea where they were being taken. Anxiously, Bracha ran out and followed them, hiding behind houses. She saw them go into the cemetery and heard her mother's wails as the Gestapo shot all three of them. When she returned to us, her face was ashen, and she was in shock. Bracha then left to be with a sister who was still living in Chelm, a larger town about 60 kilometers away.

After this horrible event, I returned to my work at the *Kommandantur*. Within a day or two of the three murders, Chaim Weintraub, a married man and father of three, was ordered to deliver a letter to the Gestapo headquarters in the village of Miaczyn, about 50 kilometers away. Unbeknownst to him, the letter instructed the Gestapo in Miaczyn to kill the messenger. When Chaim handed them the letter, they took him into the woods and shot him. Three days later, another man by the name of Avraham Tsigel, was ordered to deliver a similar letter. We warned him not to go and begged him to hide. However, because there was nowhere to hide and because he had no hope of survival, Avraham decided that he might as well be killed sooner than later. He could no longer take all the pain and suffering. As we had predicted, Avraham delivered the letter and met the same fate as Chaim.

These were some of the cruel psychological games the Germans played to dehumanize us before murdering us.

CHAPTER SIX

The Uchanie Ghetto

During the time that I worked for the *Kommandantur*, I heard that the people from Horodlo, including my mother and my siblings together with the Jews from all the surrounding villages and towns, had been taken to the Uchanie ghetto, about 19 miles away. We also heard that forty-five of the Jewish men in Uchanie had been taken to the cemetery and shot; twenty-two of those men had been from Horodlo. We were told that the Germans did not want to waste bullets, so they lined up several men of equal height and murdered them by shooting one bullet through their heads in succession. The others stood witness. As bodies fell to the ground, the remaining Jews had to bury them before meeting the same fate. At the end of this grotesque massacre, there were only two men left, Shmuel Rosenfeld and Yankele Zajdel. The Germans allowed both to return to the ghetto to report what they had seen to further terrify the Jews in Uchanie. When the two messengers returned, they were covered in so much blood, Yankele's mother did not recognize her son. It was only a reprieve for Shmuel and Yankele; later, they too were murdered.

We also heard reports that there was a shortage of firewood in the Uchanie ghetto, so the inhabitants were not able to cook the few potatoes they managed to scavenge. People were starving.

Approximately four weeks after our transport out of Horodlo, those of us who remained were also ordered out. In exchange for some of the money that the Budniewskis owed me for the armoire, I secured about 25 kilograms of potatoes and a log of wood. The Budniewskis promised that they would send the rest of the money once they knew where I was going. I trusted them.

Again, the gentile farmers prepared their horses and wagons and were waiting for us in the marketplace. I loaded my things onto a wagon, and we all began to leave the town in one long caravan. We did not know where they were taking us, and we had hardly left before the Germans ordered us off the wagons and chased us the rest of the way to Uchanie. It took us an entire day to travel the 30 kilometers on foot.

I arrived in Uchanie to find my mother, my two brothers, and my little sister all pale and emaciated. I cannot describe what it was like to see my family again. It felt to me as though they had returned from the dead. We all hugged and cried bitterly. My sister made me promise that I would never leave her again.

As for my other fellow *lantsmen* (Jews who come from the same hometown) from Horodlo, it was shocking to see how much they had changed in the four-week period since they were driven from our town. The men's beards had been shaved off, which not only greatly altered their appearance, but because of the Jewish law prohibiting men to be clean-shaven, caused much humiliation. Furthermore, the shrunken bodies of all the men and women were jarring evidence of their starvation.

My mother was elated when she saw the potatoes and wood that I had managed to bring. She had been risking her life by sneaking out of the ghetto and going into the woods to gather branches and twigs to light the stove. She knew a few people who had been caught and killed doing the same thing. My mother still had some bread that the Budniewskis had given her when she was forced to leave Horodlo, but it was full of mold.

Every morning she distributed a small slice of moldy bread to each of us, pocketing her portion. I later discovered that she was giving away her slice of bread to a woman named Sura Yita, who was all alone in Uchanie. Sura Yita had lost her husband and her only son to typhus while they were still in Horodlo. I objected to my mother giving away her bread because I felt she needed to remain strong for the rest of us. My mother claimed that since we still had some watery potato soup and Sura Yita had nothing, she would continue to give this woman her portion.

CHAPTER SEVEN

The Final Road (Dem Letstn Veg)

We lived together in the Uchanie ghetto in squalid conditions for several weeks. Then, at 5 o'clock in the morning on June 10, 1942, almost three weeks after the Jewish holiday of *Shavuos*, all the Jews in the Uchanie ghetto were ordered to gather in the marketplace. The children were commanded to wear nametags around their necks so they could be identified. This was the systematic approach of the Germans – everything planned and perfectly orchestrated.

It was a warm spring day as we all gathered in the Uchanie marketplace. This is inscribed in my memories, my nightmares. My mother was holding the children to protect them. People were crying.

The sun rose through the horizon and spread rays of light across the world as night turned into day, as though the entire world was the same, and nothing unusual was happening. With alarm on our faces and panic in our hearts, we stood in fearful anticipation, knowing what was awaiting us. Even the children seemed to know and were unusually quiet. Mothers cried silently and held their children tightly while they softly begged for a little bread. Hunger occupied the minds of the ghetto Jews, even as they waited for what they expected would be their final journey. The only other sounds we heard were the occasional sigh of the sick and the question, "What will happen to me if I'm too sick to go?"

Suddenly, murmurs cut through the silence; the Germans were coming. From afar, we saw a large group of Germans on horseback, whips in their hands. A cold sweat drenched my back at the sight of their murderous faces. To protect us, my mother gathered us in her arms and held us tightly. We moved closer together and tried to hide in each other like sheep gathering around their protective shepherd in fear of an approaching wolf. Then we heard the order, "Everyone onto the wagons!"

The Germans had ordered the Polish farmers to transport the Jews and they seemed happy to do so. Everyone started running to secure a wagon and the Jews from Uchanie who knew the farmers were first to secure seats. Since we were from Horodlo, we did not know any of the farmers and could not find someone to take us. Farmers were passing us by and picking up the Jews that they knew. Suddenly, a farmer stopped in front of us and offered us a ride. As we were climbing onto the wagon, a woman with two children approached and asked if the farmer would take her as well. The farmer agreed. We started to head out of town, thousands of Jewish men, women, and children. Since there was no room in the back of the wagon, I sat in front with the farmer and he told me about his family and his sick wife.

Soon after we left the town, the farmers chased all the Jews off the wagons and beat them, claiming the loads were too heavy for their horses. The farmer we traveled with did not order us off. Eventually, the woman accompanying us, my mother, and I volunteered to climb down and walk alongside the wagon while the children stayed on. About halfway to the train station in Miaczyn, near the outskirts of a town called Tomashov, we stopped to rest while the farmers fed their horses. I was sitting on the ground with my mother and some of the other girls and boys when our coachman approached and asked to speak to me in private. I was curious, so I followed him. He told me that he had devised a plan to save my life.

He offered that I remain on the wagon when we arrive at the train station. He would then cover me with straw and take me home to his family. He told me that he would tell the neighbors that I was a niece who had come to help his sick wife. I turned down his offer, not wanting to be separated from my mother and siblings again.

As we proceeded along the road, we encountered some young Jewish boys and girls walking in the opposite direction. They had been selected for a forced labor brigade and were returning to Uchanie from the train station. They begged us not to go to Miaczyn, warning us that going there would mean certain death. They screamed at us to run and hide. "*Gayts nisht! Ir gayt tsu a zichoron toyt!*" (Do not go! You are walking toward certain death!)

Stricken with hopelessness, we knew there was nowhere to run or hide. German soldiers on horseback were guarding us and the Poles were certain to return us to the Germans if we were found escaping. On the road, some Poles came out to whip us. We had no choice but to keep moving forward. The day was brutally hot and sunny and the extra clothing that we wore was becoming burdensome, so we began to remove layers of clothing to lighten our load. As I looked around, I saw masses of people walking with me, emaciated, hungry, worn, and weak. We all looked like dead people waiting to return to our graves. I was sad and scared. *No one could help me but God.*

The sunny day quickly turned ominous; a violent storm suddenly drenched us, while turbulent winds blew so hard that the horses tore themselves out of their harnesses and many of the wagons overturned. Our driver, the woman with us, my mother, and I tried to cover our wagon with a canvas tarpaulin to protect the children and prevent them from falling off. People were screaming and crying, their voices muted by the howling winds. We were fortunate to find shelter in a barn. Inside, there was a Polish woman milking her cows. My mother begged her to allow us to purchase some milk with the few zlotys we had left. The woman refused and left the barn with all her milk.

Amidst all this tumult, I prayed that God had purposely created this storm to interfere with the Nazis' brutal scheme. I remember raising my eyes to the heavens, the words *"Shema Yisroel"* (Hear O' Israel) escaping from my mouth. I was hoping for a *nes* (miracle*)* that somehow this tempest would stop the Nazi extermination machine; that the horrors we were experiencing would cease. I prayed with all my heart that God would intervene and stop this utter madness that had consumed my world. I walked and prayed.

When the storm subsided, we found ourselves on the same road, marching toward death. We were now dragging ourselves forward, our wet and soggy clothes becoming heavy and oppressive. Too young to comprehend the gravity of our situation, my little sister begged for a change of clothing, but all we had was what we were able to take from home in the knapsacks I had sewn from rags.

It was in this horrible condition that we arrived at the train station in Miaczyn – the transit point to Sobibor. We were hurried off the wagons, the Germans lashing some of us with their whips, which I fortunately escaped. They ordered us to leave all our belongings on the side of the road, informing us that our possessions would follow later. We were only allowed to keep the knapsacks on our backs. Men were separated from women and children. Lined up in four rows that stretched further than the eye could see, we were ordered to stand perfectly straight. Anyone sticking out of the line was whipped. Suddenly the Germans opened fire, spraying us with bullets. We were standing so tightly together the dead had no place to fall. This murderous process was repeated at different intervals while we waited in line at the train station. Standing motionless, I repeatedly touched my mother, my younger brothers, and my sister to see if they were still alive.

Around dusk, my brother Yosele, who had so recently become a *Bar Mitzvah*, asked my mother if she had brought his *tefillin*. When he heard that they had been left behind with the mountain of baggage, he suddenly slipped out of our row to retrieve them. On seeing this, my mother and I froze with fear, certain that he would not return. To this day, I cannot understand how he managed to find our parcel among the thousands of others, place the *tefillin* under his jacket, and make his way back to us without being noticed. I was so upset when he returned that I grabbed him by his lapels and shook him, called him *golem* (stupid) and said, "What were you trying to prove? Did you want us to witness your execution?" He simply raised his blue eyes to mine and answered, "No, I am not stupid! If I am still alive tomorrow morning, I will need to have my *tefillin!*"

We continued to stand in our rows throughout the whippings and shootings until the cattle cars arrived. It is impossible to adequately describe the mayhem that took place at that moment. Through a loudspeaker, the Germans ordered all the women and children onto the trains except those between the ages of sixteen and twenty-five. I was the only one in my family in that age bracket. The Germans began shooting at the Jews as they hurried them onto the cattle cars. The doors were so high above the ground that mothers were dragging and lifting their children, trying to pull them on. The pregnant women and the sick had difficulty boarding. All around, bodies belonging to those unfortunate enough to have been struck by the German bullets were sliding off the train cars. Everyone was screaming.

I stood paralyzed with fear, not knowing what to do. I wanted to go with my mother and my siblings. I did not want to be separated from them. There was no time to say goodbye. In this state of panic and confusion, I quickly asked my mother what I should do. "*Vus zol ikh ton?*" She told me to obey the Germans because to disobey would bring me certain death. Then she added, "Stay! Perhaps one *zecher* (remnant) will remain from my family."

Just at that moment, my mother removed her earrings – a pair of gold monogrammed earrings – and pushed them into my hand. She had dipped them in wax to conceal their worth since the Germans were confiscating valuable jewelry. She grabbed my siblings and headed for the train. It all happened so quickly.

My mother did not have a choice; she had to get on the train.

It was surely heartbreaking for her leaving me behind once again. She made the split-second decision to try to save me. I do not know why. I suppose she reckoned that since I was now her oldest child, and the only member of the family old enough to work for the Germans, I had the best chance to survive on my own. Nothing had been planned and the future for all of us was uncertain.

The monogrammed earrings that Freda's mom pressed into Freda's hands when they were ultimately separated.

I stood among the others who remained, watching in horror as my mother struggled to push my brothers and sister onto the train. I saw from a distance that a friend, Matel Szak, was helping my siblings climb aboard. Before getting on the train, my mother turned to pick up her knapsack that contained a piece of bread and a bottle of water, and I saw a German aim his gun at her. I could not restrain myself. I started screaming as loudly as I could, *"Momme! Loyf! Momme Loyf!"* (Mommy! Run!)

When the German heard my shouts, he turned the gun on me. At that exact instant, a girlfriend from my town named Frimmet Rosenfeld, pulled on my knapsack to quiet me down. Just as she tugged at me, the bullet flew past the side of my head. The German saw what had happened and made a motion with his hand as if to indicate that my time would come, and he did not have to bother shooting me again.

I attribute my survival to a series of miracles such as this one.

During this distraction, my mother managed to climb into the cattle car. The clanking noise of those train doors locking is forever embedded in my brain. I can still hear them today. This was the last I saw of my mother and my siblings. It was June 10, 1942, *Kaf Hay Sivan, Taf Shin Bet* in the Jewish calendar.

The trains departed and I was so distraught that I sat in the field together with the others who remained, and we all wailed. There were some other women – the old and the sick – who had stayed behind because they were too frail to board the trains. Their bodies, clothed in rags and hunched over from exhaustion and fright, were camouflaged by the heaps of knapsacks left behind by those who had been taken away. The Germans went around kicking the parcels to make sure that there were no people among them. Each time they found a person, we heard a gunshot.

All the men who had come with us to Miaczyn were left to wait for the next transport. I watched in horror and grief as they were ordered to bury the dead and clean up the area in preparation for the following day's arrivals.

To my astonishment, as I sat with the others, I saw the rabbi of Horodlo, my mother's uncle, Rabbi Moshe Yehuda Leib Halevi Berman[1], searching among the women for his daughter. He did not find her but found me instead. He offered me his daughter's belongings; I refused them, telling him that I did not know what fate awaited me, and that I was not taking my parcels either. This was the last time I saw the rabbi.

This was not the only tragedy that befell a rabbi in my own family that year. Although he was originally from Horodlo, my great-uncle Rabbi Moshe Gelernter, my *bubbe* Ziesl's brother, spent most of his life in Radzin, almost two hundred kilometers away, with the Radziner Rebbes. My great-uncle was a second cousin to the Radziner Rebbe, Rabbi Shmuel Shlomo Leiner, of blessed memory. In 1942, the Radziner Rebbe, who was also known as the "*Partisaner* Rebbe" due to his clandestine activities with the Polish resistance, came to the attention of the Germans because the Rebbe was encouraging Jews to disobey the Nazi orders and to go into the woods and fight.

Knowing that the Germans wanted to kill him, the Radziner Rebbe, along with my great-uncle, fled Radzin for the town of

---

[1] Rabbi Moshe Yehuda Leib Halevi Berman is the author of *Tiffereth Banim, The Responsa, Chok Moshe, Zichru Torat Moshe,* and *Kol Yehuda.*

Wlodowa, about eighty kilometers away, and went into hiding. It was not long, however, before the Germans discovered that the Radziner Rebbe was in Wlodowa and ordered him to give himself up. If he refused to come out of hiding, they threatened to kill all the Jews of Wlodowa. Without telling the Rebbe about the situation, my great-uncle went to the *mikvah*,[2] put on his *kittel*,[3] *tallis*,[4] and *tefillin*[5] and presented himself to the Germans as the Radziner Rebbe. The Germans immediately dragged him to the cemetery while the Polish people stood cursing, spitting, and throwing things at him. My great-uncle, Rabbi Moshe Gelernter, posing as the Radziner Rebbe, was shot and killed by the Germans in the Wlodowa cemetery.

When the Germans discovered that Rabbi Moshe Gelernter had deceived them and that the Radziner Rebbe was still alive, they were furious. They again threatened to kill all the Jews of Wlodowa unless the Rebbe came out of hiding. The Jews who were helping to hide the Rebbe had no choice but to tell him everything that had transpired. He cried bitterly when he heard the terrible news. Had he known, he would never have allowed my great-uncle to sacrifice his life for him.

This time, Rabbi Shmuel Shlomo Leiner, the Radziner Rebbe, who had already lost his wife and six children to the murdering Nazis, went to the *mikvah*, and dressed in his *kittel*, *tallis*, and *tefillin*, presented himself to the Nazis. In his case, too, the Poles laughed at him, spat at him, and mocked him, as he was being tortured and dragged to the cemetery. Then he, too, was murdered in the same cemetery in Wlodowa.

---

[2] A *mikvah* is a ritual bath used to achieve spiritual purity.

[3] A *kittel*, which denotes purity, is a white robe worn by Orthodox Jewish males during High Holiday services and Passover. It is also worn by grooms under the wedding canopy, and it is used as a burial shroud.

[4] A *tallis* is a fringed prayer shawl.

[5] Phylacteries

The Final Road (Dem Letstn Veg)

Front row left: Rabbi Tzvi Hersh Gelernter, the son of Rabbi Moshe Gelernter. Front row second from left: The Radziner Rebbe, Rabbi Shmuel Shlomo Leiner. Behind these two rabbis: Rabbi Chaim Halevi Berman, the son of the Horodlo Rav, Rabbi Moshe Yehuda Leib Halevi Berman.

CHAPTER EIGHT

The Selection

The morning after I last saw my mother and my siblings, we were ordered to line up in single file at the train station in Miaczyn. From afar, I saw three Gestapo officers at the front of the line commanding people to go either to the left or the right. I wanted to pray to be sent to the good side, but I did not know which side to pray for. As I drew closer to the front, I realized that most of the fragile, old, and sick people were being sent to the right. I saw that when siblings were separated and begged to stay together, they too were sent to the right. I noticed that there were far fewer people on the left side, and they all appeared to be younger and stronger. Trembling, I mumbled a prayer to *Hashem* (God) that I would be sent to the side that meant life. My friend Frimmet, who had saved me from the German bullet when my mother boarded the train, was standing immediately behind me. Hearing my unintelligible mumblings and thinking that I was losing my mind, she patted me on the back and said, "Please, Fradale, hold on to your senses because we are standing between life and death." I assured her that I was not crazy and that I had just been praying.

My turn came to stand before those German butchers. They confiscated my document and sent me to the left. Frimmet was sent to the right. Watching my beautiful friend walk to the other side from where I was standing, and sensing that I would never see her again, I was overcome with the deepest sorrow.

At the end of the selection, all those on the right, including my friend, Frimmet, were brought to a Nazi camp near the town of Chelm. Yankele Zajdel, my friend who had survived the previous killings at the cemetery upon first arriving in Uchanie, was among them.

News of the horrific conditions in this camp near Chelm – the Jewish inmates were forced to parade naked – was brought to us by Yankele, who joined us once again after managing to escape. He made his daring getaway with a friend named Itchele, who was the grandson of Moshe Boimel, another family friend. Unfortunately, when one of the Ukrainian guards realized that the two had run away, he hunted the two escapees. Catching Itchele, this Ukrainian evildoer brought him back to the camp, and hung him publically for all the Jewish prisoners to see.

We, the remaining Jews who had been sent to the left, were ordered to stand in four rows. Escorted by the Germans, we were marched down the road toward Uchanie, all the while being savagely whipped by the soldiers. The people who were targeted were walking closest to the guards; I was lucky to have been on an inside row beyond their reach. A young bespectacled man walking next to me in one of the outside rows was less fortunate. The soldiers whipped him so ferociously across his face that they broke his glasses and lacerated his skin. As blood oozed from the gashes on his face, this young man continued to march without uttering a word. He was so stoic that he did not even cry out with pain. Instead, he quietly whispered to me, "Please, whoever is walking next to me, take my hand. I cannot see and if I stumble, they will surely kill me." I took his hand and led him through this cruel ordeal.

We walked down roads and through Polish villages and eventually our German military escorts disappeared. We were no longer ordered to march in fours. People dragged themselves forward at their own pace, scattering in fear whenever we passed the Polish farmers on the road. We could have run away, but what was the point? There was nowhere safe to go. I had no expectations that our Polish compatriots would have sheltered us owing to the dire ramifications to them and their families. However, I was disgusted that many of them were complicit in assisting the Germans in chasing down and killing Jews. This, no doubt, added to the multitude of Jewish deaths in Poland. I often think about the staggering number of Jews killed during the war and how different the outcome would have been had the Poles not so eagerly colluded with the Germans.

After trudging along for what seemed to be quite a long time, we saw a German officer, resplendent in his uniform, riding in a horse and buggy with a beautiful Jewish woman sitting next to him. It was rumored that she had worked for him in Uchanie before the transports and had been ordered to Miaczyn with the rest of us. Apparently, he had followed her to Miaczyn and somehow managed to get her back. As we walked, he rode next to us and, to our surprise, offered to carry our knapsacks to lighten our load. He was quite a bit ahead of us when a Polish farmer suddenly darted out and grabbed one of the boys marching with us. The farmer pulled the young Jew into his yard and started beating and whipping him while his wife stood watching from the porch. We all started screaming and eventually the noise reached the German officer. Immediately, the German backtracked to where we were standing, jumped off his wagon, and chose two other boys to assist him in carrying the bloodied boy back to his wagon. He then grabbed the farmer's whip and beat the farmer fiercely, saying, "Now you will feel the boy's pain!" I am not sure if the German killed the farmer, but when we left, the farmer laid still on the ground. At that time, it was astonishing to witness a German with a modicum of decency.

Upon our arrival in Uchanie, we found the *Judenrat* and a few Jewish families still living there. This was the pattern of the Nazi slaughterers. They would leave a few favored families behind in each town to give the appearance that Jews can remain alive as long as they continue to cooperate with the Nazi occupiers. These remaining

Jews in Uchanie took us into their homes and fed us. Afterward, we were split into groups according to the towns from which we came, and each group was given a house, most likely abandoned by Jews, in which to spend the night.

Before nightfall, I left to see the house where I had stayed with my mother and siblings. I found it locked but managed to crawl in through an open window. Inside, I spotted my mother's down coverlet, along with my sister's little wool hat, and my brother's *tzitzis* (ritual knotted fringes). I found my mother's glasses and her *siddur* (prayer book) with the yellowed pages soaked with her tears. In the kitchen, I recognized some of the potatoes and the log of wood that I had brought from Horodlo and a few of the branches that my mother had collected from the forest for firewood. I lay down on the branches and cried bitterly.

I do not know what happened; I must have blacked out. I awoke at daybreak and found my arms wrapped around those branches. I took the *siddur*, the hat, the *tzitzis*, and the down coverlet. Amazingly, I still have my brother's *tzitzis* and the coverlet; my little sister's hat proved to be useful in a subsequent unanticipated event. I then climbed out the window and headed back to my assigned house to join the others. My housemates were shocked to see me; they were sure that I had been killed. In fact, they were so sure that I was dead that they had eaten my portion of dinner and breakfast. They were apologetic and offered me some of the little remaining food.

We were given new work identification cards, indicating that we were *"dringend benötigt"* (urgently needed) for work. Having this card represented life; death came quickly to those without jobs. The card was so valuable that I always carried it, even when I slept. Along with the work identification card issued to me by the *Kommandantur* in 1939, these artifacts are powerful reminders of how I survived.

Once we had our identification cards, we boarded two wagons driven by local farmers and headed out along a road. To my surprise, after traveling for about three hours, we arrived back in Horodlo, entering the town at the same time that the gentile population was

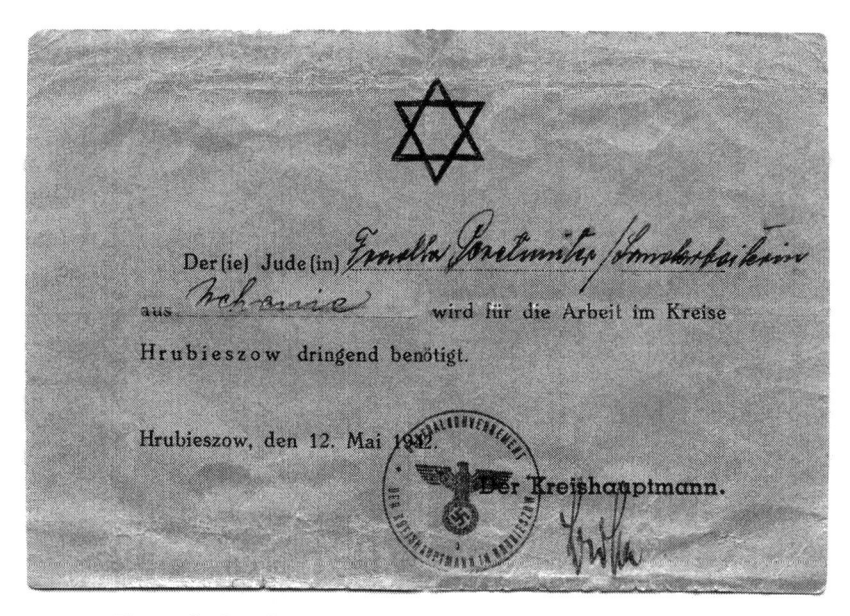

The work identification card issued to Freda in Uchanie in 1942.

leaving church after Sunday services. As soon as they saw us, the gentiles reacted with hatred and hostility, gathering around us and staring as if they were spectators looking at circus animals. There was one exception: Katya Budniewska, the woman who had baked bread for my family before our transport. She seemed genuinely happy to see me and greeted me with hugs and kisses. She did not care that the other gentiles were looking at her with malice, malevolence, and disbelief. *How could she be hugging and kissing a Jew?*

Given the chance, some of the angry onlookers would have gladly revealed a Jewish hiding place in exchange for a bag of flour. Moreover, they were afraid that we might try to reclaim our houses and the possessions that we had left with them for safekeeping. I could understand that aiding a Jew meant risking their lives, but the Poles did not have to help the Germans kill Jews. Although I know from my own survival that some were truly righteous gentiles, most were collaborators who had the chutzpah to claim *they* were victims of the Nazis. After seeing how my fellow Poles treated the Jews, I vowed that if I survived, I would never return to Poland – and I never did!

That same day we received our new orders from the mayor of Horodlo at the behest of the Germans: we would be taken to Starzeń, an estate approximately seven kilometers southeast of Horodlo that had been owned by a wealthy Polish prince before it was taken over by the Germans.

CHAPTER NINE

Starzeń

We arrived at the Starzeń estate toward evening. It was hard to believe that it had been only four days since the devastating events in Miaczyn. To our surprise, we found a few Jewish people already working there who had originally come from Warsaw. There were also a few Jews from the nearby village of Strzyżów, including Hersh Mostysser, a girl named Sarah Fox, her two brothers, Shmuel and Aaron, and a man named Velvel Sznol. Hersh and Sarah, whom he later married, and her two brothers survived the war, and we remain friends until today. Velvel survived the war and returned to Strzyżów to stay with a Polish friend to whom he had left his house and possessions. One morning, he and his friend were found decapitated.

There had been Polish workers in Starzeń who had been hired by the prince to farm his land and had been given houses and property. When the Germans took over Starzeń, they retained these Polish workers and one of them was assigned to supervise us while we worked. Once again, the Polish gentiles were happy to lord over helpless Jews. The estate grew sugar beets, and we were given the labor-intensive job of beet leaf control — manually thinning out the densely-planted crops with a hoe during growing season, leaving only one single leaf for each beet plant. Hunched over between two rows of beet greens and swinging our arms from side to side, we used hoes to cut the greens, then put down the hoes and ripped the beet leaves out of the ground with our bare hands. This process made room for each beet plant to grow. We worked from dawn to dusk, stooping the entire day, with virtually no food. There was no shade to hide us from the blistering sun that beat down upon us. Those who did not complete their quotas were beaten and ordered to work into the night. We were given a break at lunchtime, but people who worried about not being able to finish their day's work did not even stop for lunch. We decided amongst ourselves that as night fell, we would help those who had not been able to reach their quota so we could all return to our barracks together.

I had arrived in Starzeń wearing the same coat, dress, and sandals I had been wearing for weeks. Since the coat made it harder for me to move freely and my sandals cut into my feet and were not suitable for working in the fields, I worked barefoot and without a coat. When we returned home, I, like my fellow laborers, had lesions and lacerations covering my hands and feet.

Despite these conditions, I worked quickly and always made sure to take my much-needed rest at lunchtime. Even when the others got ahead of me in their work, I knew that I would catch up by the end of the day.

While I was resting at lunchtime one day, two Gestapo officers arrived on motorcycles. As soon as I saw them, I ran to my place in the field and rushed to catch up with my work. I grabbed the hoe and quickly began cutting the weeds to catch up with the others. The officers focused their attention on me and stood scrutinizing my work as I labored with vigor and precision. After about ten or fifteen minutes, one of the officers poked me in the back and with a shout of *"Halt!"*, directed me to stop working. When I did, he glowered at me for what felt like an eternity and then both officers mounted their motorcycles and rode away. I later learned from the Polish supervisor that the two Gestapo officers had timed my work and were astounded to see how fast and flawlessly I labored. The supervisor then announced to our group: "Today, Fradl has saved a life." The Nazis had come for the sport of killing a few Jews and were searching for a victim who could not keep up with the work. Monitoring my work had distracted them from finding someone who could not work as well.

* * *

On the first night back in our dilapidated housing, we had nothing to eat. The boys went out and managed to find a stale heap of barley that the farmers had discarded. They also discovered a large, rusted metal pan, which we cleaned and used for cooking. With difficulty, we cleaned the barley as much as we could to get rid of all the mud. Shaindel Rosenbloom, the oldest of our group, assumed the role of cook. With her guidance, we cooked the barley with water heated with straw that burned so quickly it had to be constantly replenished. Our faces and clothing were so blackened by the soot that we looked like chimney sweeps. The barley took an exceptionally long time to cook.

The next day, to our surprise, we received a package of meat, only to find out that the meat had come from a deceased horse. Everyone, except for me, devoured the food. I refused to eat meat from a dead horse and furthermore, I was still trying to keep kosher. It was only after the war I learned that eating non-kosher food was permissible if it meant saving my life.

A few more days passed with continual backbreaking work and little food. I was starving. All I had to eat was the "barley soup" and a few meager pieces of bread that Shaindel still had in her knapsack. One evening I came home so exhausted and hungry that I broke down and cried. The pain of the unfathomable loss of my family, together with my fatigue and starvation, was destroying me. I had been so focused on my survival; I did not allow myself to grieve the loss of my family. The helplessness I now felt in not being in control of any aspect of my life compounded my despondency.

When my wracking sobs ended, I resorted to what had always

helped me – prayer. As I had done many times in the past, I invoked the name of Rav Pinchas Shapira of Koretz, a renowned Kabbalist and ancestor of mine, to intercede on my behalf before God. The rabbi had left a *tsevuah*, a decree, imploring his descendants to call out his name, and that of his mother, Sarah Ruchel Shaindel, whenever we were in distress and he would then petition the Almighty to protect us. I would later pass on the story to my children, who on many occasions found comfort invoking the rabbi's name.

I prayed, recalling the words of the blessing recited after meals: "*Na'ar hayiti, v'gam zakanti v'lo raiti tzadik ne'ezov v'zaro me'vakesh lechem*" (I have been young, now I am old; and I have not seen the righteous forsaken nor their children begging for bread).

Miraculously, at that very moment, Chana Rosenbloom, Shaindel's sister, entered our barracks and disclosed that Matewka Budniewski was in Starzeń looking for me. *Matewka in Starzeń?!* I thought, surprised by her announcement. Before finishing her sentence, Matewka appeared at the door with a parcel. He had brought me bread, butter, salt, knishes, and onions. I could not believe that he had found me and brought me this lifesaving food. It was truly a miracle. We all stood looking at the food in astonishment. I was so stunned that I could not find enough words to thank him. He told me that the Gestapo was still in Horodlo and that I should not try to come back there. He promised that he would return the following Sunday. He was staring at my bare, swollen feet, and my tattered clothes, and said he would try to find me clothing and shoes.

Matewka kept his word. He returned on Sunday, bringing with him more food, high-laced shoes, and a man's jacket. I could not have endured much longer without these gifts. Matewka requested a picture of me, which I luckily had among some of the family pictures I had managed to bring with me in my knapsack. I did not question why he needed my picture but realized that he had a plan. He told me he would return the following Sunday. Before he departed, I mustered the courage to ask him to bring linen rags and disinfectant. Some of the boys in our group had deep, infected leg wounds and I wanted to help ease their pain.

As promised, Matewka returned with more food, clean rags, and the disinfectant solution I had requested. These visits and gifts from Matewka saved my life. I probably would have died of starvation or disease if not for his kindness.

Matewka brought a gift of a different kind along with the food and supplies. He told me that the Gestapo was preparing to leave Horodlo. I would never have considered returning to Horodlo while the Gestapo was there.

The next day we received information from friends at another camp that the Gestapo had indeed left Horodlo. We did not work on most Sundays, so on those days we would risk taking hazardous trips back to our hometowns in search of food and goods. On one such occasion, Mashala Friend was caught in Horodlo by the border patrol, taken to the cemetery and shot. Frightening as this news was, we continued our Sunday journeys. Most of the time I would return to Horodlo with my friend, Fradl Bloom. The seven-kilometer trek was arduous. We would walk through the wheat fields and the pastures, across the dilapidated Jewish cemetery, through the Christian cemetery, and past some orchards to avoid walking on the major roads. We would stop for bread at the house of a farmer named Nowosat and then make our way to the Budniewski home. Before the war, Fradl's father, Yitzchak Bloom, had owned a bakery and had done business with Nowosat. I knew Nowosat's oldest daughter, Olga, from public school. For seven years she sat next to me, and during exams, I slipped her the answers to help her pass.

On one such trip to Horodlo, I was sitting on the porch while Fradl went inside to see Nowosat. I could hear Olga and her friends laughing and listening to music and see them dancing through the porch window. When Olga came outside to get some fresh air, her face turned crimson. Infuriated at seeing me, she ran back into the house, slamming the door. She had supposedly been my friend, but now I heard her tell the others that there was a foul-smelling Jew polluting her porch.

I was so hurt by Olga's insults that I cried the whole time as Fradl and I made our way from Nowosat's house to the Budniewski home. When we arrived at the Budniewskis' farm, Matewka was outside in his yard. Seeing me crying so hysterically, he ran over thinking that I had been beaten. I recounted the story of what had happened with Olga. Knowing that her father was such a decent man, he could not believe it. He then said to me, "Do not cry. You never know what can happen. *You* might outlive *her*!"[1]

Fradl and I continued our trips to Horodlo on our free Sundays. To enter the Christian cemetery, we had to remove one of the vertical slats of the gate surrounding it. One Sunday morning, we entered the cemetery to find a group of gentile boys and girls flirting. Our town was small, so I knew them all. When we saw them, our gut reaction was to retreat, but they had already seen us. They started shouting at us, saying that we were so dirty that we brought dishonor to the dead in the cemetery. They spat at us and cursed us. We tried to ignore them and continued on our way.

When I would go to the Budniewskis, Matewka's mother often greeted me outside with some bread and vegetables hidden in her apron. She would implore me not to tell Katya, her daughter-in-law, about her gifts to me. The elder Mrs. Budniewski had known my entire family. Before 1918, when Horodlo was occupied by Russia, there had been a fire in Horodlo that destroyed many of the houses, among them my mother's family home. At that time, Budniewski's father, Anton Budniewski, was the *burgermeister* (mayor) of Horodlo and a great friend of my maternal grandfather, Leibel Zawidowicz. He helped my grandfather salvage whatever they could from the fire. Furthermore, my grandparents and their children, including my mother, lived in Anton Budniewski's house for a year while they

---

[1] Indeed, I found out much later that Olga had died suddenly at the age of eighteen, only about six months after I saw her, on Christmas Eve 1942. She died of a stomach illness caused by overeating kielbasa, a Polish sausage, and drinking to excess.

rebuilt their house.

In addition to being a close friend of ours, Anton Budniewski was a true friend to the Jews. On one occasion, he proved his friendship during a pogrom when one of the Cossacks had a Jew trapped under his horse and the Jew was about to die. Some of the Jews ran to Anton to report what was happening. He immediately left city hall and ran to the marketplace, where he ripped open his shirt and standing bare-chested yelled at the Cossack, "You will have to kill me before you kill this Jew!"

Eventually, despite the request from Matewka's mother, I felt that I owed it to Katya to be honest with her and told her about her mother-in-law's gifts of food to me. She smiled and admitted knowing all along.

***

We continued to work in the sugar beet fields until the summer harvest when we were assigned the arduous tasks of reaping and harvesting wheat. There were only fifteen of us working in the wheat fields, performing work that normally required many more laborers. Two tractors drove through the fields cutting the wheat and our job was to gather the cuttings and bundle the stalks into sheaves, tying them at mid-center with straw. We had to chase the tractor to keep up the pace of tying the bundles with the tractor's cutting. By the time we had finished binding one row, we had to quickly run back to the starting point because the second tractor had already begun cutting.

Without any cover to shade us from the sun, our skin blistered. Thorn bushes growing between the wheat rows made the job more difficult and painful. The straw we used to bind the bundles was full of thorns that punctured our palms and caused our hands to swell. Those who did not have shoes and worked barefoot suffered cuts on their feet. I was extremely fortunate to have the high laced shoes I received from Matewka.

We loaded the wheat bundles onto wagons and brought them

to the barns. Once the barns were full, we had to stack the wheat outside the barn, making a mound the size of a building. As the mounds grew higher, we used ladders to pile the haystacks. To make our lives more difficult, the ladders had been taken away by our Polish supervisors, and so we had to jump to get down. I was always the first girl to jump with the boys. When we reached the bottom, we made piles of straw to cushion the fall of the girls who were afraid to jump.

By this time, I was wearing two handmade leather wrist splints that I had received from one of the gentile farmhands. Without these splints to contain the swelling and pain in my wrists, I could not have continued for much longer.

***

While at Starzeń, in August 1942, I received a postcard from the city of Lvov (Lemberg) from my dear fifteen-year-old cousin, Chanale (Hanka) Zawidowicz:

Dear Fradziu,
I am letting you know that I became an orphan just like you. My momme and my sister, Sala, left on August 10, 1942, in the same way your mother had left. I remained with my mother's friend. I am not short of food, but I am very unhappy. Now Mrs. Schechitowa has come to us. I have not received word from Warsaw, and I am very worried. If you write to our bubbe, ask her in my name to go to our grandfather, Leibel, and inform him about everything. Write to me often because I am very lonely, and your letters make me happy. Be well.
Yours,
Hanka.

On the front of the postcard:
I do not know anything about my dear father.

It was not difficult for me to decipher Chanale's cryptic

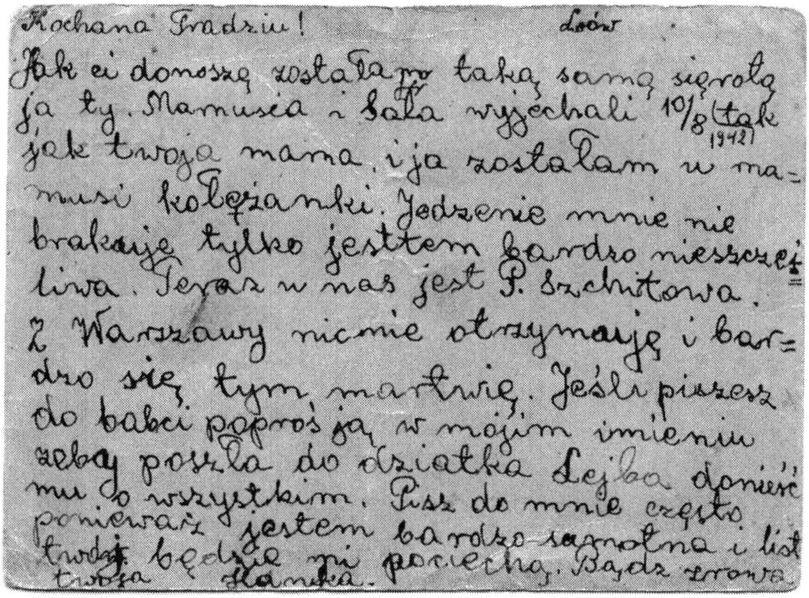

Starzeń 71

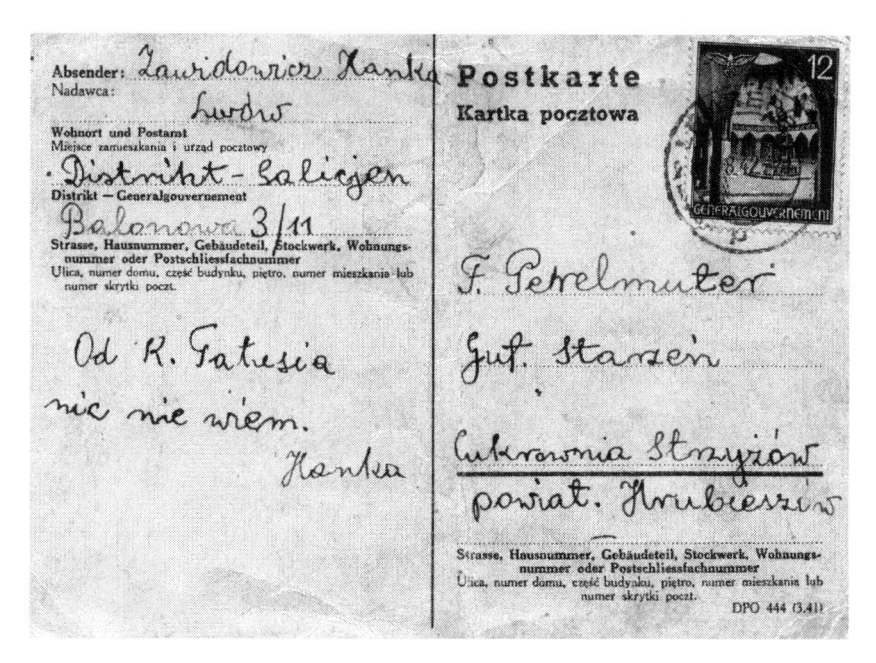

*Cryptic postcard from Freda's cousin, Chanale (Hanka) Zawidowicz.
August 1942.*

message. I immediately understood that her mother, my aunt Malke, and her sister Sala (Surale), had been taken to the death camps. Moreover, Mrs. Shechita (the slaughter lady) was a pseudonym that she used for the Gestapo, yet her characterization fails to represent the extent of their systematic and barbaric efforts to exterminate the Jews. Chanale's reference to her lack of communication with Warsaw cast a doubt on the status of our two uncles, who had settled there. Further illustrating her dire situation, she encouraged me to write to our *bubbe* Ziesl to request that she go to the grave of Zeide Leibel and pray for her safety. Although she confided to me that she had heard nothing from her father, I already knew at the time that he had been murdered.

This postcard, which I have kept all these years, was the last communication I had with my young cousin, Chanale.

* * *

Throughout my time at Starzeń, I continued my journeys back to Horodlo on my free Sundays. One week, as Fradl Bloom and I took our usual path through the cemetery, we found a Protestant pastor waiting by the fence, curious to see who kept breaking it. He lived in a house near the cemetery that had previously been a Polish school. He invited us onto his porch and, although we were nervous and disinclined, we went with him. My friend and I sat on the porch while he went inside, hoping that he might bring us some food. He returned empty-handed and instead invited me to come in to see his house. In the hope of obtaining food, I followed him in with great trepidation, unsure of his intentions. When we were inside the house, the pastor revealed to me that he had heard from the mayor that the remaining camps in the area were going to be liquidated and that we were all going to be killed. The pastor apprised me of his plans to leave Horodlo. He informed me that he had taken notice of me during my visits to my friend Bracha Blat, who had once been his neighbor. He added: "You are blond with blue eyes and do not look Jewish. I know that you come from a prestigious, rabbinical family. I come from a family of pastors, and I am willing to save your life on one condition – that you become my wife."

Shocked by his proposal, I immediately refused him!

He was clearly astonished and said, "Are you telling me that you would rather die than convert?"

"If that is God's will, so be it," I answered.

Without uttering another word, I bolted out of his house and my friend and I quickly departed.

CHAPTER TEN

Escape

The farmlands in Starzeń stretched for miles across the estate, so we were driven to them by horse and buggy. One day, on the way to the fields, I was riding on the wooden ladder used to mount the wagon, holding onto its frame. As we went down a hill, the wagon suddenly overturned onto the side where I was sitting. Everybody escaped with some bruises, but I fractured my right elbow and wrist. I did my best to control the agonizing and pulsating pain. After the wagon was righted, they loaded me back onto it and we returned to the estate manager's office. The manager, wanting to help me, said that he would arrange for a driver to take me to Hrubieszów, where I could get some medical care. To make it safer for me, he would give me a special permit that would allow me to ride on the wagon. I looked him straight in the eyes and asked, "Will this permit save me if I am stopped by the Gestapo on the way to Hrubieszów?"

"I don't know," he answered.

The thought of traveling all the way to Hrubieszów, almost twenty kilometers away, in an open wagon with a broken arm terrified me. Instead, I asked him to send me to the nearby village of Strzyżów, only six kilometers from Starzeń, where there was a non-certified medic who I thought might be able to help me. The manager agreed, adding, "Don't worry. I will not send you away and I will not make you work until your arm is healed. I know that you are the best worker in this group, and I will still give you the same portion of food as the rest." I thanked him and left for Strzyżów.

Unfortunately, the medic in Strzyżów also advised me to seek professional medical assistance in Hrubieszów. Expressing my fear of traveling to Hrubieszów, I appealed to him to do the best that he could with my arm. He tried to reduce the elbow fracture, twisting it back into place. The pain was excruciating but I did not cry out. He was shocked at my silence, wondering how I could keep it all in. I explained that the bitter fate of my family was much more painful to me than my broken arm. Then, he casted my arm with the only plaster he had left and told me to return in two weeks.

Back at the barracks I was in tremendous pain, and I was terrified that the Gestapo would come and check for the sick and the frail. I could not remove my dress without cutting it off me – and because I did not have a replacement – I slept in my clothes.

My fears became a reality the following week when our cook, Shaindel Rosenbloom, raced in to inform me that a Gestapo officer and his dog were searching house to house for the sick. There was no escape. Hurriedly, she assisted me into my bed and covered me with the down comforter I had brought from Uchanie. On top of the comforter, she spread a blanket to smooth out the surface of the bed. She did the same on the bed next to mine to make it look as if the beds were made. The Gestapo officer did not enter the house. He stood at the door and peeked inside while Shaindel was cooking in the kitchen. I was terrified for my friend as much as for myself. When he saw that the beds were made and that the house was neat, he left. Incredibly, he did not suspect I was there and his dog did not sniff me out. I could not have stayed under those covers for very long because I did not have much air. Once again, I miraculously survived.

The next day, I put my arm in a homemade sling and went out to work with the others. I did not want to risk getting caught in the

The Rosenbloom sisters (and others) in 1938, on the engagement of their brother, Yosef. Third from right: Shaindel Rosenbloom. Fifth from right: Chana Rosenbloom. Seventh from right: Fradl Rosenbloom. Second from left: Yosef Rosenbloom and his bride (first person on the left).

barracks. When the Polish foreman saw me, he pointed his finger at me and said, "You will be the first of this group to be shot!"

I worked in this manner for two weeks until I returned to Strzyżów to see the medic. He removed my cast, placed two wood boards on my forearm and wrapped it in bandages. I was instructed to soak my arm in warm water and begin exercising it. I returned to the work camp with my broken arm wrapped in bandages. Bringing my hand to my face was impossible, so I used my other hand for the minimal hygiene I could manage.

Despite my fractured arm, I continued to work until the harvest season was nearly over. On October 19, 1942, we received an order from the Germans that we would be taken to Hrubieszów the following day to perform some other type of work. True or not, I believed that I did not stand a chance of survival with my broken arm. My only chance was to escape and find a hiding place. In the middle of the night, I decided to flee Starzeń for Horodlo, hoping that the Budniewskis would help me.

That night a torrential rainstorm made it impossible for me to navigate my usual back roads. Under cover of darkness and rain, I walked the seven kilometers to Horodlo through the main streets, hoping to go unnoticed by the German patrol. There was a downhill road that led from the marketplace to the Budniewskis and the downpour was so great that I sat and rode the current all the way to the bottom.

When I finally reached the Budniewskis' house I was surprised to find them awake and dressed so late at night. As it happened, they had already heard from a relative, who was a Nazi sympathizer, that my work camp was going to be liquidated the next morning. They hoped I would somehow make my way to them – but Matewka was prepared to come for me if I did not.

Matewka had prepared a hiding place for me five months earlier, in May, before harvesting the hay. Katya explained that she had a dream in which my mother appeared, begging Katya to save her last surviving child. They told me that they wanted to help preserve the legacy of the illustrious family from which I came.

Matewka's mother, Katerina, who lived with them, was asleep when I arrived and never learned of my presence on their property. Matewka and Katya did not share their secret with anyone. I know it was painful for Matewka to keep the secret from his mother. In the summertime, she preferred to relax in the barn, which was cooler than the house, and could never understand why Matewka made her go inside for lunch. Later, while I was in hiding, I heard her complaining to her friends that she could not make sense of this change in her son. Matewka used to write to me that he hoped she would live long enough to tell her the truth. Unfortunately, she died before he could.

I was blessed to have this righteous couple, Matewka and Katya, rescue me. Many Poles, I later found out, turned in Jews to escape punishment or to obtain a reward of money or scarce goods. Others were motivated by antisemitism. I had an advantage over other fleeing Jews because I knew and had faith in this family. Other

Jews could not be sure if the Poles they looked to for refuge would save or denounce them.

The Budniewskis gave me something to eat and, before they led me to the barn, I grabbed both their hands and cried. I was trembling. "I have nothing to offer you for your kindness," I told them, "but I will pray that you will have a child." Despite being married for ten years, Matewka and Katya had no children of their own and this was the greatest gift I could imagine for them.

Then, in pitch darkness, they took me to the barn. That night I slept on top of the haystack that extended almost to the roof of the barn. The next morning Matewka took me to the hiding place that would be my home for the next twenty-one months.

CHAPTER ELEVEN

Hiding

It is impossible to adequately describe the horrors of my nearly two-year solitary confinement beneath the earth.

Matewka had dug a hole under the haystack in the rear left corner of his barn and a long, narrow, underground tunnel that stretched from the left side near the barn entrance to this hole. He had constructed a wooden frame around the inside of the hole and tunnel that included a makeshift ceiling to prevent the earth and haystack from collapsing on me. The hole itself was small, no larger than a twin size bed. I could lie down flat, turn from side to side, and sit up in a straight leg sitting position, but I could not dangle my legs. Standing was impossible.

The ceiling of my hideout extended above ground by the height of three slats of wood, through which I could get some light and air and glimpse outside. The floor of my pit was covered with hay upon which Matewka had placed a linen sheet. I also had a pillow and a down comforter. There was a little wooden shelf above my head where I kept some food, a bottle of water and, eventually, a small mirror. Food and water were brought to me by way of the narrow tunnel through which I first entered the hole.

The entrance to the tunnel was hidden by a plug of hay that perfectly matched the rest of the haystack. For additional protection,

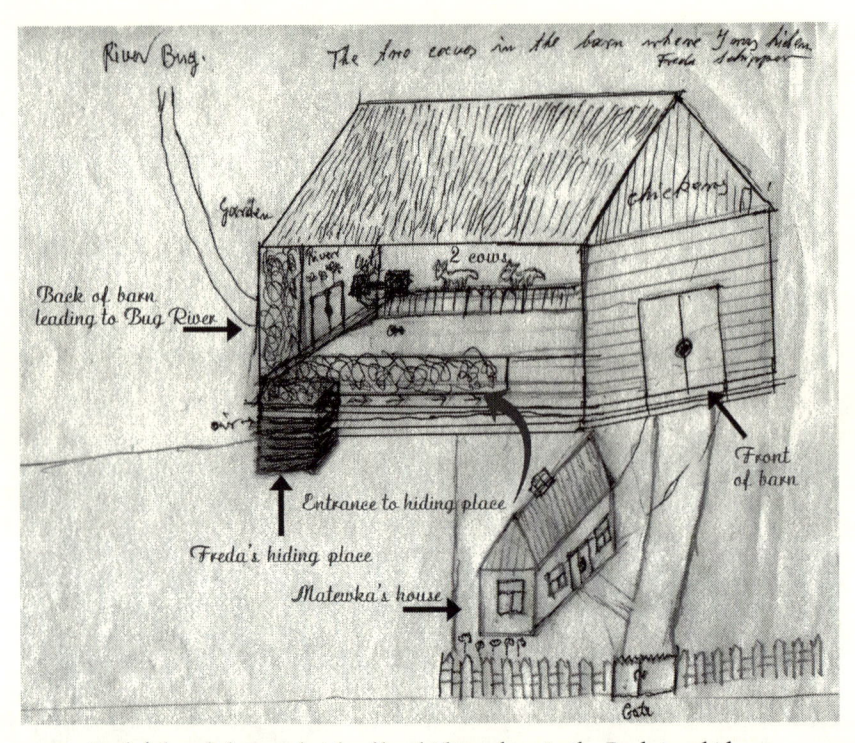

Freda's hand-drawn sketch of her hiding place in the Budniewski barn.

Matewka had placed a small pile of firewood in front of the plug. When he brought me food, he would knock three times on the pile of wood to announce his presence, move the wood aside and remove the plug of hay. Upon hearing Matewka's signal, I would crawl on my belly into the tunnel to retrieve the food and water. During these exchanges, I handed him the pot I used to collect my waste, which he would empty, wash, and return to me. I never saw Matewka's face, only his hands. We never spoke for fear that someone might overhear; we would communicate by touching hands or passing notes to each other. This was how I learned what was happening in the outside world.

My hideout was usually very dark, but I could see daylight through the three highest wooden slats and hear the conversations of the peasants in the street. It is through this crack between the slats that I learned of the bitter fate of my friends from Starzeń; most were shot in an empty field in Hrubieszów on October 20, 1942, one day after I came to the Budniewskis. A small number managed to escape but were unable to find a safe place to hide or anyone willing to help them. Poles discovered them hiding in their haystacks and turned them over to the Germans. My dear friends were summarily executed. Among them were three of my *lantsmen* from Horodlo: Fishel Shok; his father-in-law, Mendel; and Yankele Zajdel.

No one can comprehend the type of anguish and grief I felt – so many good, decent, honest people murdered only because they were Jews. Reflecting on these events, I realized what a blessing my broken arm turned out to be. Had I not been so debilitated by the fractures in my elbow and wrist, I would have continued my work in Starzeń and perhaps I too would have been brutally murdered in Hrubieszów.

When I first entered the hiding place that Matewka had prepared for me, the cows with whom I shared the barn sensed my presence and mooed continuously in protest. I was terrified that the cows would betray me to the merciless Poles or Nazis. To my relief, the cows grew accustomed to my scent after a few days and settled down.

My first several months in hiding were grim and frightful! I would try not to sleep during the day so I could sleep at night. My bones were aching, and sometimes my limbs felt paralyzed from disuse and poor positioning. There was little I could do. I was terror stricken – Germans were searching for Jews and threatening any gentiles who dared hide them. I could hear the Poles outside the barn discuss how hidden Jews were being forced to leave despite large payments that the Jews had made to their Polish hosts. Each time I heard Matewka arrive, I feared that he was coming to tell me that he had changed his mind about hiding me.

As the days and weeks passed, my apprehension that the Budniewskis might panic and let me go intensified. One morning, after approximately four months in hiding, Matewka passed me a note with incredible news. Katya was pregnant after being childless for ten years! He asked me to pray for good health for her and their baby. For me, this was reassurance that they had no intention of telling me to leave. They believed, as I did, that *Hashem* answered my prayers and was finally granting them their first child as a reward for helping me.

The days dragged on endlessly and I cried bitterly day and night. Before I went into hiding, I was only concerned with staying alive, but now I had endless time to think about the horrible deaths I imagined that my entire family had suffered. I was no longer afraid of dying, but the possibility of being caught and tortured terrified me.

Maintaining my cleanliness, to the extent possible, was a high priority. During the summers, I sponge-bathed as best I could, using the water that I had in the pit. I cleaned my hair by scrubbing my scalp with a wet cloth, and I put about one quarter of a teaspoon of kerosene into my hair to keep it from tangling and to prevent lice. Then, I braided my long tresses and wrapped the braids around my head to keep it clean. I wore a little kerchief to protect my hair from debris falling from the hay. In the beginning of this almost two-year period of isolation, I did everything one-handed because of my broken arm. During the winters, it was too cold to wash, but I continued to receive clean clothes and sheets about once a month from the Budniewskis.

I tried to keep occupied by exercising my broken elbow and wrist, placing my elbow against the wooden slats, and using the weight of my body to try to straighten out my arm. I had asked Matewka for a crochet hook, and he fashioned two hooks out of stainless steel that I used to crochet and exercise my

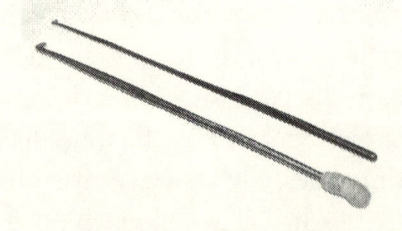

Crochet hooks, handcrafted by Matewka, used by Freda while in hiding.

wrist. I still possess the two crochet needles Matewka fabricated for me. Later, when the Budniewskis' daughter was born, I crocheted a little vest for her reusing the yarn from my little sister's hat, the one I had brought from the house in Uchanie.

During the day I would catch a glimpse of the outside world by peeking through the cracks of the three uppermost slats of wood forming the outer wall of my hole. With the little bit of light that penetrated my hiding place, I struggled to read and write. I kept a diary and wrote poems with the pencil and notebooks that Matewka provided.[1]

Sometimes at night I would peer through the slats of wood just to glimpse the outside. One night, I heard a commotion coming from the home of our neighbors across the way. They were hysterical over the death of one of their cows. I witnessed the family cutting up the meat and packaging it to sell the next day. I quickly penned a note to Matewka, informing him of what I saw and urging him not to purchase the contaminated meat from the neighbor. Would these neighbors ever have suspected that an underground Jewish spy was observing their secret? I felt satisfied that I was able to offer Matewka this useful information.

Once, I wrote a note to Matewka asking him for a pocketknife that I could use to sharpen my pencil when the nib dulled. Otherwise, I had to put my writing on hold until the time that Matewka

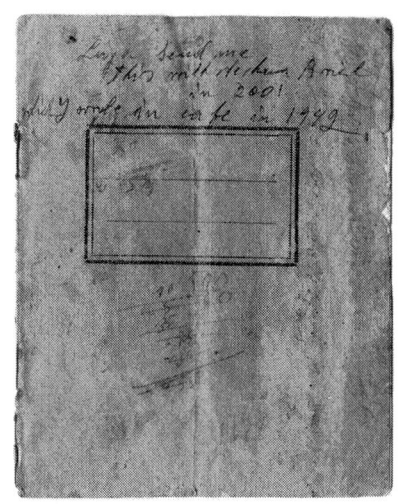

Notebook containing the Yiddish and Polish poetry that Freda wrote while in hiding. 1942-1944.

---

[1] My poems survived but my diary was later destroyed by the Poles, who raided the Budniewskis' house when they tried to kill him after the war. A collection of my poems was published in Yiddish and Hebrew in *Di Kehila fun Horodlo* or *Kehilat Horodlo*, a *yizkor* (memorial) book, which can be found online and at the Jewish Public Library in Montreal, Canada. The reader can find Freda's poems, translated into English, in Appendix 1.

could sharpen my pencil and return it to me. His response came quickly and decisively: "I'm not that stupid!" He was scared that at some moment – and there were moments when I was longing to die – I might take my own life. He would not provide me with any tools that I could use to kill myself if I could no longer cope.

Freda's poems in Polish

Hiding 87

Freda's poems in Yiddish

Since Matewka only had access to Russian and Ukrainian books, I taught myself Russian. Matewka had given me a Polish–Russian letter chart and I learned the language by reading books in Russian that I had previously read in Polish. One of the books was *Anna Karenina*. A second book was the Bible.[2]

During the period that I was in hiding, the Germans demanded taxes from the farmers, which were paid in wheat. Many of the farmers hid the amount of wheat they had under the hay in their barns, so the Germans went searching the haystacks with pitchforks. Once, they came to check the Budniewskis' barn. Luckily, it was shortly after the hay had been brought in from the fields so the stacks above my pit were extremely high. Nonetheless, I was panic stricken, and my body shook uncontrollably as I heard the Germans poking around above me in the barn. *Is this my end? Will this be the way I die?* Thoughts of my impending death filled my head, and I was immobilized with fear. Katya had left that day to stay with her parents because she was afraid that such a scare would cause her to lose the baby. Matewka stood outside in his garden, ready to flee if they found me. Hiding in my pit after the Germans left, I thought about how close to death's door we all had been.

Living in the pit, I shared my quarters with rats, mice, and other vermin, and I inevitably found myself facing another challenge – fleas! My makeshift bed was infested! There were hundreds of the little black insects under my covers and I had bite marks all over my body. I was itchy and in pain. I would lie in that tiny space and cry, feeling punished in so many ways. Whenever I lifted my cover, I could see hundreds of them, but as I soon as I tried to get them, they would scatter.

As the weather grew colder, I discovered that the fleas were immobilized by the cold, which enabled me to start killing them

---

[2] Knowing how to read and write Russian proved to be extremely useful after the war when the Budniewski family was driven out of Poland into the Ukraine, and I needed to correspond with them and their children.

one at a time. One day I killed two hundred. I crawled out from under my cover every day to wage my war on the fleas. After about a week, I did not find a single flea under my comforter.

Sometime in January 1943, around my twentieth birthday, I received a small, wrapped package with my food. In it was a little *siddur* (prayer book) that contained the signature of our neighbor's little boy, Shapsale Szek. He had been a friend of my brothers and they had often played together. Matewka wrote that he had found this *siddur* among a pile of Jewish books that had been discarded by some Poles when they were taking over Jewish homes. How correct he was in thinking that this would be a wonderful present for me. And indeed, it was! I prayed from it daily while I was in hiding.

That January it became so frigid in my hiding place that even the feathered comforter could not keep me warm. I was afraid I might freeze to death and sent a note to Matewka telling him so. He gave me the quilted lining from the inside of his coat, which I used to sew a hood for myself using a needle and thread Matewka had provided. This angel also gave me his fur coat and instructed me to place it under the comforter for additional warmth. When I crawled down the tunnel to fetch my food, I covered the fur with my comforter to prevent the heat from escaping. Even my bottled water started to freeze. When I poured the water into a small bowl, it froze, and I used this ice to clean my hands.

In contrast to the freezing winters, the summers were so brutally hot that the drinking water in my bottle was near scalding. I often fainted from the extreme heat. If Matewka knocked on the woodpile and I did not respond, he would stick a long pole down the tunnel and poke my feet until he felt me push the pole back with my hands. In this way, he would determine, to his relief, that I was still alive.

A year after I went into hiding, Katya gave birth to a daughter, and they named her Liya. At the christening, the priest asked the Budniewskis from where they had gotten the name, as there was no such Christian name. Matewka satisfied the priest by explaining that he was so happy to have a child after ten years, that he named her after the lily flower, Lilia. In truth, the Budniewskis had given their daughter the Jewish name, Leah, believing that Liya's birth was a direct outcome of their decision to save me and my prayer for them to have a child.

CHAPTER TWELVE

Germany Retreats

The Bug River ran behind the Budniewskis' property. Since the river was now the border between Poland and the Soviet Union, the German border patrols cut through the Budniewskis' barn to reach it. During the day, when people were about, I was not concerned that they would hear me under the barn. However, I was terrified that I would cry out while sleeping or that even the slightest cough would be audible in the quiet of the night.

Once, I had a vicious cold and was coughing relentlessly. Matewka sent me a letter saying that he was worried that his "hidden cannon had started to fire!" To protect me, he decided to sleep on the haystack above me in the barn. Whenever I started coughing, he coughed too.

A German soldier who was passing through the barn to reach the border heard the coughing, stopped, and shouted, "Who's there?"

Matewka looked down from the top of the haystack and answered, "It's only me."

"What are you doing sleeping in the barn?" the soldier asked.

Matewka wittingly replied that he had fought with his wife, and she had thrown him out of the house. The German was laughing so hard when he left that I heard him all the way to the river.

***

In the brutally cold winter of 1943–1944, German advancement into the USSR was halted by the Soviet forces and driven back. The Germans conceded they were no match for the harsh Soviet winter and the indomitable Red Army. The German retreat was good news – it was the first sign that the tide of the war was turning.

For me, however, that winter was an even more harrowing time. As they retreated to the Bug River, the Germans commandeered all the barns in Horodlo to house their horses for a new offensive. The Germans occupied the barn in which I was hiding. Their horses began eating what was left of the hay that was not already consumed by the Budniewskis' cows. Matewka feared my hiding place would be revealed.

In May 1944, Matewka decided to cut the grass and store it in the barn without letting it dry in the sun, which was the traditional way of making hay. The neighbors became suspicious, knowing that he had brought the hay in too early. When they asked him why he had done that, he told them that, not knowing what the war would bring, he wanted to ensure his animals would have food. All the farmers then decided to emulate Matewka and bring the green grass to their barns as well!

As the Germans retreated toward Horodlo with the Red Army in pursuit, I faced a new set of dangers. German and Soviet planes were shelling and bombing the area. Wounded soldiers were left on top of the hay in the Budniewskis' barn until they could be taken to medical facilities. Matewka feared that I would fall asleep, and the wounded soldiers would hear me. He told me to try to stay awake, and I tried, but by then I was so weak and tired that staying conscious was almost impossible. I was hardly eating anymore, and my bones were visible beneath my thin skin making me look like a living skeleton. Fortunately, after a few days, the injured soldiers were dispatched elsewhere.

CHAPTER THIRTEEN

Hell Beneath the Earth

As the bombing and shelling intensified over Horodlo, setting houses and barns ablaze, Matewka prepared another pit for me. Beneath where the cows were sheltered, Matewka dug a tunnel that stretched from under the barn foundation to an underground hole outside the barn where his corn crops were growing. Once again, he supported the hole with wooden slats and placed some hay in the hole along with some water, food, and a small lamp.

Matewka decided to transfer me to this new pit because he was afraid that I might be trapped if the barn caught fire. He helped me relocate to my new shelter and handed me a military shovel, telling me that I should dig myself out once I hear that the Soviets have entered the town or if the barn begins to burn. Hearing this I imagined trying to scratch my way out of a tomb to avoid being buried or burned alive. Nonetheless, I went into the new pit and Matewka covered the entrance with a box of manure.

To this day, I cannot comprehend how Matewka managed to dig this new hole and tunnel with the Germans swarming all around. *How did he go unseen? How much time did he have? Where did he put the earth that he removed? How did the Budniewskis maintain the courage to put their own lives at risk to save mine?*

My new hiding place was much smaller than the old one and

deeper in the ground. I could not even straighten my legs. It was like living in a grave and I did not have much air to breathe. I was in total darkness and disoriented. I did not know whether it was day or night. I lost all track of time. The little lamp that Matewka gave me would not burn because the wick was too short and there was not enough kerosene. To raise the level of kerosene, I decided to urinate into the lamp, in the hope that the level of the kerosene would rise high enough such that the wick would light. I was petrified that the kerosene would overflow onto the hay, which would ignite as soon as I lit a match. I placed my index finger over the rim of the lamp and used it as a level indicator to prevent spillage. I decided to risk striking a match to light the lamp, but the match was too damp to ignite so I placed it in my bosom to dry. I do not know how long it took, but I finally got the match to burn long enough to light the lamp. After all that, the lamp only lasted about two hours.

Time seemed to stretch endlessly in the darkness. I heard the loud roar of countless planes overhead and the violent thunder as bombs detonated all around me. The Germans were operating a cannon that was in the yard adjacent to where I was hiding and every time they fired it, the booming noise was so deafening that I lost my hearing for a while. The earth tremored in response to the constant pummeling and dirt fell into my hideout.

I lay in this dark hole in the ground in a crouched position, weak, sick, and unable to eat, without any sense of how much time was passing. At some point – I do not know whether it was day or night, possibly it was the next morning – a storm erupted. The rain was so heavy that water started filling the hole I was lying in. The tunnel filled first and then the water started rising in my pit until it eventually reached my chin. I was faced with the horrifying prospect of drowning in a sea of mud. I tried to get to the tunnel but could not get past the mud. Helplessly, I sat in what was becoming a sludge-filled grave. There was nothing for me to do but pray for deliverance, so I prayed for God to rescue me as he had saved Abraham from Satan's River at Mount Moriah *(Midrash Tanchuma, Vayera 22)*.

As quickly as it had begun, the storm ended and the water miraculously began to recede. I was not going to drown, but something was wrong. I felt that I was wasting away from malnutrition and immobility, and now I could feel warm fluid oozing from my nose and mouth. I heard someone in the barn milking the cows. When I saw that the tunnel was only half-filled with sludge and realized that I would be able to keep my head above it, I climbed into the tunnel and, lying on my belly, slithered through the muddy tunnel under the barn and quietly knocked on the box of manure that covered the entrance. Katya, who was milking the cows heard my knock and I heard her say to the cows, "Stay, let me milk you. What happened to you? Let me finish milking you." I knew that she was talking to me so I returned to my hole and waited. I felt my life ebbing. I knew that the chance of my survival in this pit was very slim.

I do not know how much time passed before I heard Matewka. He probably had to wait for the Germans to leave the barn. When he removed the box, I was already waiting there for him. I wiped my face with my hand and smeared it on his hand. He saw that his hand was covered in blood. I begged him to return me to my previous hideout. To risk being burned to death in the original hideout was preferable to staying in that "grave."

Matewka said that he would come back to help me as soon as it was feasible. When he returned, he took me out of the pit and helped me back into my previous hiding place. He had to carry me because I could no longer walk on my own. When he left, I did my best to clean the mud from my body and the dried blood from my face.

***

As the frontlines of battle approached Horodlo and the Germans prepared their offensive from the Bug River, the people of Horodlo were ordered to evacuate the town. They were told that the destruction from the imminent military offensive would wipe the entire town off the map. Everybody left, including Katya.

Horodlo became a ghost town; only I remained under the earth, or so I believed.

As the houses and barns in Horodlo continued to burn and the people evacuated, Matewka told me to prepare to leave my hiding place in case his barn caught fire. He had already removed the firewood in front of the straw plug at the entrance to my tunnel so that I would only have to remove the plug to escape. Knowing that I could not walk, he told me that he was leaving one of his cows so that if I needed to escape, I could hold on to the cow's chain for support. Were anyone to ask why I had not already left Horodlo, Matewka instructed me to say that I was too ill to leave and had been left behind.

By this time, I was totally exhausted, ailing, emaciated and helpless, and now I felt thoroughly alone. The booming noise of the relentless shelling and the exploding bombs intensified as the fighting between the Germans and the Soviets raged. I was the only one left in Horodlo, *one soul beneath the earth*. Forlorn, I could no longer curb my feelings of hopelessness or quell the voice inside me screaming that this might be the end. I feared dying in this pit, vanishing from the world, as if I had never existed, with no one ever knowing my story. Having all my energy sapped, I closed my eyes and tried to fall asleep, no longer caring what would happen to me. Whatever it was, I wanted it to happen while I slept.

CHAPTER FOURTEEN

Freedom

I awoke at dawn to an eerie silence as the sun began to rise in the sky. There was no shelling, no bombing, no sound whatsoever other than birds chirping. This deafening silence was so unusual and in this most peculiar way, I felt that I was finally free. I kept asking myself, *could this really be the end of my suffering? Is this nightmare finally over?*

I had no idea at the time what day it was but later I learned that the date was July 24, 1944. Horodlo was still intact, but no one was around. The Soviet army, it turned out, had entered Horodlo from an unexpected direction that caught the Germans by surprise, and many were taken prisoner.

Approximately a half hour after I awoke, Matewka arrived and told me that the Red Army had liberated the eastern part of Poland where Horodlo was located. This was approximately one year before the war ended. I told Matewka that I was surprised he had made his way back to Horodlo so quickly – no one else was in the town. He surprised me by revealing he had never left. During the evacuation he stayed behind distributing glasses of milk to the German soldiers who were advancing toward the river, a useful excuse for him to stay in the town. One German officer asked Matewka why he was aiding them and Matewka replied that as a German patriot

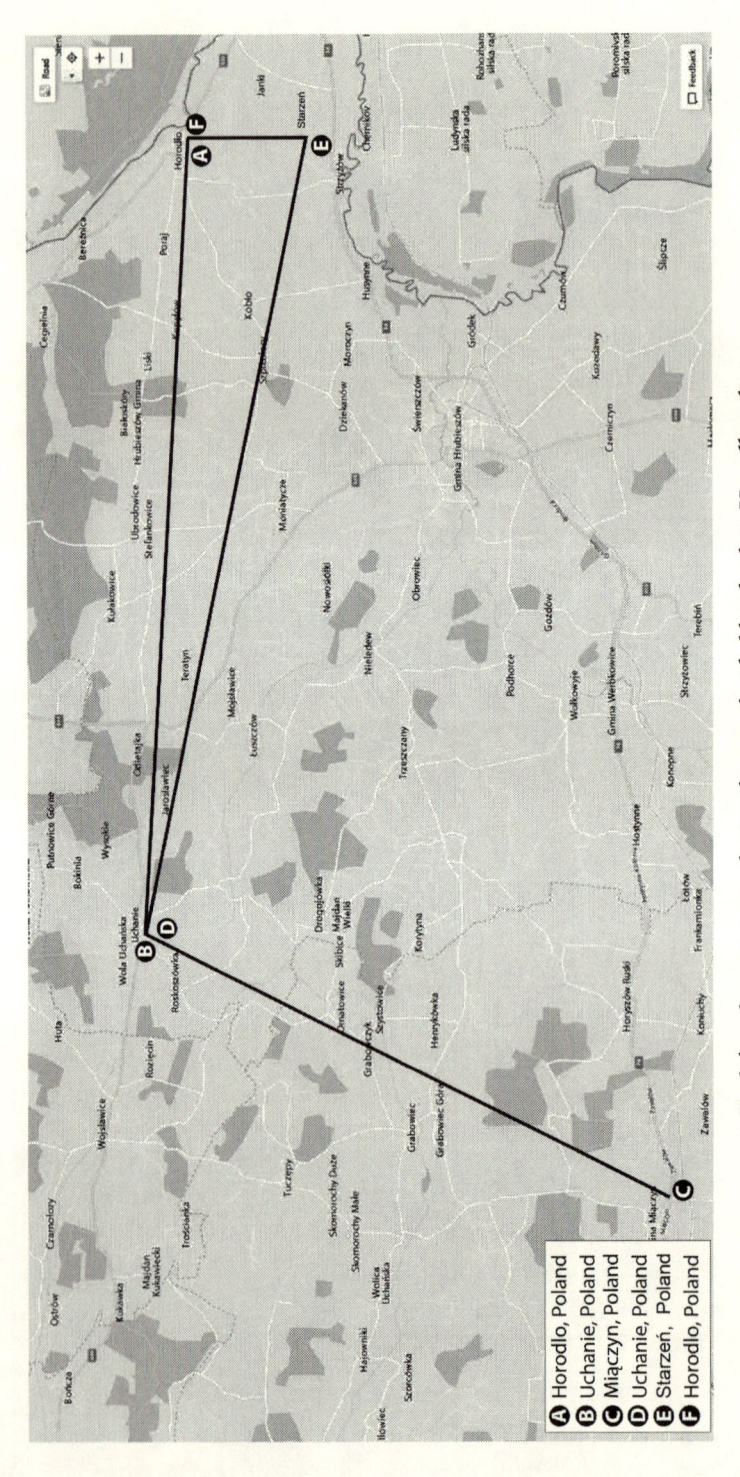

Freda's arduous journey during the war that led her back to Horodlo, where she was saved by the heroic actions of Matewka and Katya Budniewski.

A Horodlo, Poland
B Uchanie, Poland
C Miączyn, Poland
D Uchanie, Poland
E Starzeń, Poland
F Horodlo, Poland

he wanted to help the soldiers.[1] Impressed with his good deed, the officer promised Matewka that he would return and take Matewka with him should the Germans have to flee. Matewka had a different plan however, and dug a hiding place for himself underneath the flowers in his garden. When the Germans began their retreat, Matewka heard the German officer looking for him but he stayed buried until the German had gone.

I remained in my hideout until that evening, crying non-stop the entire day. I thought about everything that had transpired for over half a decade – the hunger and starvation, the forced hard labor, the witnessing of indescribable atrocities, and my nearly two years of solitary confinement beneath the earth. The searing torment burned inside me like molten lava flowing from an erupted volcano. All I could think of was that my entire family – over 85 people – had been murdered. *I am all alone.* I thought to myself. *To whom do I belong? Where is my family? My beautiful mother? My pious and hardworking father? My three brilliant and loving brothers? My adorable little sister? My grandparents? My aunts? My uncles? My cousins?* How I would have given anything at that moment for one of their hugs, to see one of their smiles, to be back in our home with everyone around me. I thought about my wonderful and kindhearted Bubbe Ziesl. What I would have given to hear some words of wisdom from her now and to hold her as she so often held me. *What kind of freedom will I have without them?* I had seen my mother and three younger siblings board the train for Sobibor. *Could any of them have survived such horrific atrocities? And my father – what happened to him after he took that perilous trip across the Bug River so long ago?* I was obsessed with thoughts of my dead family and all the people I had ever known. I could not fathom a life without them. Every basic truth of life that I had known – my home, my family, my friends, and my sense of safety, had vanished into thin air. *How would I live?*

---

[1] This was plausible because the Ukrainians had aligned themselves with the Germans during the war.

Toward evening Matewka returned to pull me from my hiding place. Although I was emotionally exhausted and physically debilitated, my spirits brightened, and happiness tiptoed into my heart as he carried me like a baby into his house. The atrophied muscles in my legs could no longer support me. I had spent twenty-one months alone, lying on hay in an underground pit beneath a barn, unable to walk or talk, barely existing. When Katya saw me, I looked so awful that she crossed herself.

Seeing Liya for the first time cheered my soul and an intense feeling of gratitude swelled up inside me. I felt an immediate, deep affection for her, the child born of my prayers. Being able to communicate freely and articulating in an audible voice felt both strange and liberating. *Can you imagine living in complete silence for almost two years?* The first sounds of my own voice startled me but at the same time I was tickled with emotion at finally being able to speak.

We all sat in the kitchen while Katya prepared supper. I was sitting on a bench near the window, holding Liya on my lap, Matewka next to me. As Katya readied herself to bring the pot to the table, a bullet pierced the window between Matewka and me. Had Katya been sitting with us she would have been killed. The bullet was meant for Matewka.[2]

Matewka ordered everybody to fall to the ground and we crawled on our bellies to the entrance of the cellar. My first night in freedom, I slept on the cellar floor with the Budniewskis and their baby daughter, Liya.

The next morning, after emerging from the basement, I was treated to a brilliant sunrise, something I had dared to dream about

---

[2] This was the second time the Poles tried to kill him. The first time had been at the onset of the war. As an ethnic Ukrainian, Matewka was the subject of animosity from the local Poles due to the long-standing tension between the two nationalities dating back to the Polish-Ukrainian War of 1918-1919. The conflict intensified between 1942 and 1945, when Ukrainians massacred Poles in Volhynia and Eastern Galicia to regain sovereignty over those areas of Poland that had a Ukrainian majority.

in hiding. As the golden rays ushered in a brand-new day, I felt a stab of hope that things would get better. It was a peculiar feeling – a numbness resulting from incredible sadness wrapped in a whisper of optimism.

Learning to walk again was challenging in my weakened state. In those first few days after emerging from my hideout, I walked around the Budniewskis' house steadying myself by grabbing hold of household items such as tables, chairs, counters, and doorknobs. Determined to get stronger, I exercised vigorously.

* * *

The Budniewskis did not want anyone to know that I was staying in their house. Matewka worried that his neighbors might try to kill him for harboring a Jew. He was concerned for my safety as well, because there were Poles murdering Jews after the war. I was therefore encouraged to remain indoors.

Despite these fears, I occasionally risked venturing out to his farmland to breathe the fresh air and walk the grounds. During those first few trips outdoors, Matewka's grazing cows came running over to greet me, displaying full recognition of their nearly two-year "barnmate." I marveled at how they knew it was me.

Soon after I came out of hiding, I discovered that only six Jewish boys from my entire town had survived the war never leaving Horodlo. I was the only girl. The boys who survived were Fishel Gertel, Leibel Berger, Leibel's three cousins, Shmiel, Aibish, and Dovid Berger, and one man by the name of Yankel. I later learned that Fishel and Leibel had survived the war together by moving from one hiding place to another.

One afternoon, Katya came in from the yard and told us that Fishel and Leibel were approaching the house. I was instructed to hide behind a door that led from the kitchen to another room in the house. Fishel and Leibel had come to ask Matewka, who had been a watchmaker, to repair their watches. While they were in the kitchen, Fishel, knowing that I used to go to Matewka's house from

Starzeń in search of food, questioned Matewka about why he had not helped save me. "If you would have saved one Jewish girl from our town, then I would have had myself a *kallah*, a bride," I heard Fishel tease Matewka. Upon hearing this, I was unable to endure the weight of this eagerly anticipated reunion with my friends. I slowly opened the door, supporting myself on the door posts. While Fishel was talking to Matewka, Leibel noticed me at the door and was so startled, he thought he was hallucinating. He stood up, ran over to hug me, and exclaimed, "*Shema Yisroel!*" (Hear O Israel!) and asked, "Are you alive or are you dead?" When Fishel and Leibel realized that Matewka had saved my life, they both dropped to the floor and kissed his feet! Matewka took out a bottle of whiskey and we all celebrated together.

* * *

After Horodlo was liberated by the Soviets in July 1944, none of the houses that had previously belonged to Jews were returned to them. The Polish government designated a few houses for the small number of Horodlo survivors to live in. My Jewish friends offered to take me with them to live together in one of these houses, but I refused. I had a great family, a good home in which to stay, and a baby girl whom I very much adored. I wanted to stay with the Budniewskis until the end of the war.

A few days after the liberation of Horodlo, Matewka's brother Wasil came to visit. Wasil had been a university professor in Volodymyr before the war. Apprehensive that the Soviets would arrest him if he remained there during the war, Wasil and his wife had visited Matewka while I was in hiding and had asked to stay. The request was natural given the close relationship between the brothers and the fact that Wasil had grown up in the house Matewka lived in. This was, after all, their parents' house. Matewka turned him away without explanation because Matewka did not want to put the lives of his brother and his family in danger should the Germans discover me. In addition, Matewka did not dare tell his brother about me because Wasil's sister-in-law was married to the mayor of Horodlo, a notorious murderer. Knowing that Wasil had the opportunity to reside with his in-laws, Matewka did not feel guilty about sending him off. Although Wasil was initially upset and disappointed, the brothers maintained a good relationship and Wasil often visited their mother at Matewka's house. Now, Matewka took his brother by the hand and led him to me, his hidden treasure. He told Wasil who I was and that I was the reason he could not allow Wasil to stay with him. Wasil immediately forgave his brother and they both cried as they hugged and kissed.

A few months later, toward the end of 1944, I was ecstatic to receive a letter from my father, Nosson Nuta Perelmuter. He had survived the war in Siberia, and settled in Bukhara, in what is now Uzbekistan, with other Jewish survivors. I can never articulate how euphoric I was to discover that I still had a father! To find my father alive after the war was yet another miracle. I would no longer be alone, no longer an orphan!

I immediately responded, telling him that I was alive but all alone. I did not foresee what a shock it was for my father to find out that I was his only surviving family member. When he had left for the Soviet Union, our family numbered over 85 people. Now, he was hearing for the first time that, except for me, they had all perished. He had not only lost his wife, three sons and one daughter, he had lost his parents, Yisroel and Sarah Leah (Szulman) Perelmuter, his two brothers, Leibish and Pinchas and their families, and three young sisters, Esther, Malke and Dina. All his aunts, uncles and most of his cousins had perished in Sobibor. There were only a few cousins who had also survived in Siberia; they now live in Israel.

I later learned that when my father received my letter and read the terrible news, he lost his will to live. He had descended to the cellar, placed ashes on his head – a Jewish sign of mourning – and refused to eat. He was just waiting to die. One of his friends, Yankele, realized that he had not seen my father for a few days and came looking for him. He found my father in the cellar almost lifeless. Yankele told my father that he too had written a letter to his family in Chelm and, unlike my father, had received no answer at all. He said, "Imagine what your daughter has lived through. She is all alone in this world. All she has is you. You must live, if not for yourself, then for her."

It took another two years before my father and I were reunited.

Freda, after liberation. Horodlo, 1945.

CHAPTER FIFTEEN

A Sad Goodbye

*E*ven though Horodlo had been liberated, my troubles were far from over. An armed struggle continued between the Ukrainians on one side and the Poles and Soviets on the other. The Ukrainians had aligned themselves with the Germans during the war and had received German identification cards, or *Personalausweis*. Matewka had taken advantage of the situation and managed to obtain a false identity card for me just in case I needed to pose as a Christian.

The Poles were driving the Ukrainians to the other side of the Bug River, out of Poland. The Budniewskis were hoping that the animosity between the two groups would subside, and they would be able to remain in Horodlo. At night, however, Poles would break into Ukrainian homes, robbing the owners and either killing them or forcing them to flee. One night a group of Poles came banging on the Budniewskis' door in search of Matewka. Matewka threatened to shoot anyone who came into the house, but the marauders managed to break through a window. Matewka climbed to the attic and took the ladder with him. The men wore masks. I assume that meant that they knew we would recognize them and that they did not want to be identified. They searched the house and when they went up to the attic, Katya and I stood paralyzed with fear that

False identification card (Personalausweis) Matewka obtained for Freda, who posed as a Christian during and after the war.

they would find Matewka and kill him. When they came down, it was clear that they had not been able to find him. Since they expected us to know where he was, they started striking me on the head with their gun butts. Clearly, they preferred to beat the Jew. Even if I had known where Matewka was, I would *never* have told them. The men beat me horribly, stole things from the house, and destroyed whatever they could not take with them. They took my only coat and my diary and left. The loss of my diary hurt me more than the blows I received.

When he was sure that they were gone, Matewka descended from the attic where he had prepared an escape hole to the top of his house. The roof was made of wooden slats and bundles of straw that held the slats together. Matewka had left one of these bundles of straw loose so that he could remove it and climb out onto the roof. Once he was through the hole, he had replaced the missing straw and laid flat on the roof while the Poles were searching the attic.

A Sad Goodbye

The next day, Matewka decided that he and his wife and daughter had to leave Horodlo. He made a deal with his Polish friend, Bielecki, who was returning from Ukraine, to take charge of Matewka's house and property. My altruistic savior also left a will stating that all his possessions in Horodlo – the house, the land, and the properties – belonged "to the girl, Fradl Perelmuter, whom I raised." I signed the document together with Matewka, Bielecki, and two other witnesses.

That day, Matewka loaded his family and his belongings onto wagons, traveled to the Ukraine and settled in Volodymyr. Seeing them leave everything behind – their house, their barn, the orchards and gardens, and about ten different parcels of land – broke my heart. Saying goodbye to the people who had risked their lives to save mine was gut-wrenching.

I never saw them again.

Matewka's will that bequeathed to Freda the house and land he owned in Poland.

CHAPTER SIXTEEN

The Danger Continues

Still suffering from the head wounds inflicted on me by the Poles who had broken into the Budniewskis' house, I had nowhere to go but to join some of the Jewish boys, who were living in a house in the center of the marketplace where Jews had lived before the war. I came to stay with Fishel Gertel, Aibish Berger, and Leibel Berger. By the time I had arrived, there were two Jewish women staying with them. One was a woman named Chana Zuberman, who was born in Horodlo and had survived in Volodymyr. Tragically, her husband and child were murdered. The other occupant of the house was a young girl, around sixteen years old, named Chipele Cigler. The boys had found her living with a farmer, and although the farmer was reluctant to let her go, they had taken her with them. She later married Leibel Berger and they settled in Israel.

Shortly after I joined my Jewish friends, a gentile woman came to the house and told us that she was in possession of five *Sefer Torahs* (Torah scrolls) that had been brought to her for safekeeping by a Jewish man. Since we were the only Jewish survivors of our town, she wanted us to have them. A few of the boys went to her house to retrieve the *Torahs* and when they brought them home, I bundled them together in a white cotton sheet and placed them in a corner of one of the rooms. I wish I could remember the name of this righteous

Freda (front row, third from left) with Fishel Gertel (front row, fourth from left) and other friends after liberation. Horodlo, 1945.

woman or the name of the Jewish man who had risked his life to bring the *Torah* scrolls to her.

We intended to stay in Horodlo until the official end of the war since we had enough contacts to ensure that we would not go hungry. Furthermore, we still hoped that some of our belongings would be returned to us. Our plan was to contact relatives or other Jews abroad in an attempt to leave Poland.

Our hopes were soon dashed – living in Horodlo after it was liberated proved to be almost as unsafe as it had been under the Germans. Although the Soviets occupied this area, they gave the Polish police the power to maintain order. When the war officially ended on May 8, 1945, Jews throughout the country remained in danger. Sadly, not a day passed without Jews being murdered by Poles. The antisemitism in Poland was deeply rooted and did not dissipate after the war.

There were still open pogroms against Jews. There was one pogrom in Rzeszow on June 12, 1945, followed on August 11, 1945, by one in Krakow. On July 4, 1946, the infamous Kielce pogrom occurred in which Polish civilians, police, and citizens killed 42

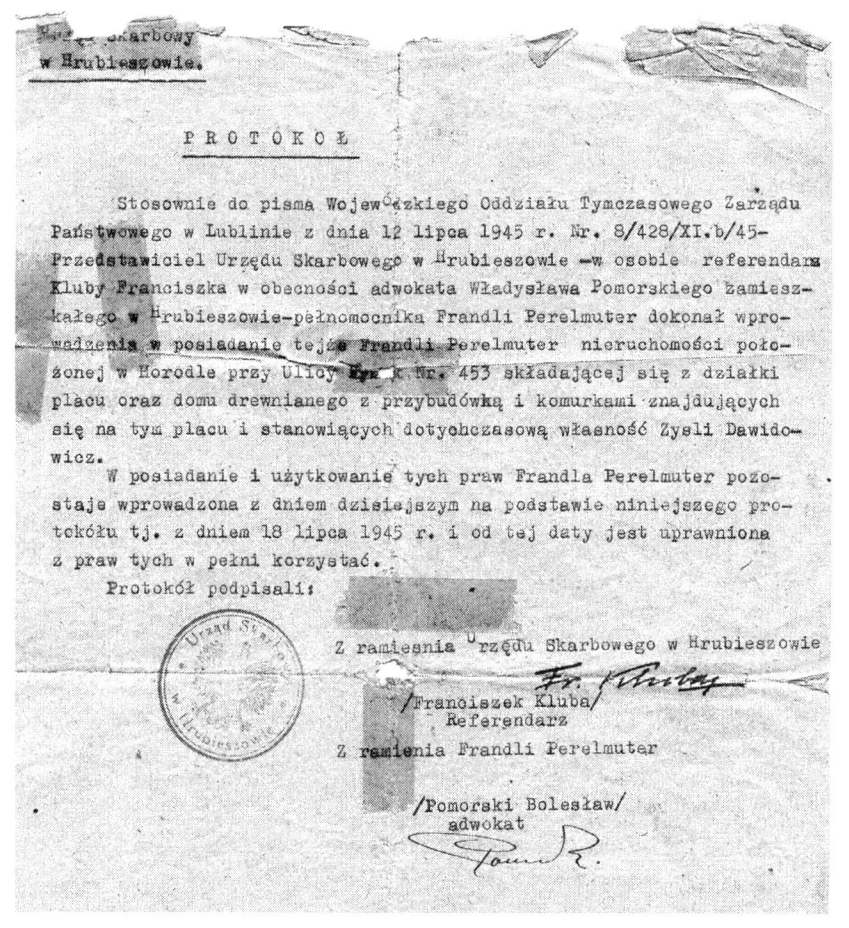

A document obtained by Freda on July 18, 1945, officially granting ownership to her of the parcel of land and house on 453 Rynek Street in Horodlo. This house, in which she grew up, had been previously owned by Bubbe Ziesl (Zysla Zawidowicz). Despite this document, Freda's property was never returned to her.

Jewish survivors and injured 40 more. All three pogroms were triggered by the ludicrous antisemitic charge of "blood libel" – that Jews needed the blood of gentile children to make *matzoh*. Mendel Schipper, the man I would meet and marry years later in Canada, and his brother Hersh, miraculously survived the pogrom in Rzeszow.

* * *

On a Sunday afternoon in the spring of 1945, a Polish woman named Luciowa came to our house to report that she had overheard a group of Polish youths in church plotting to murder us that night. We could not determine whether she was telling us the truth because we had lost confidence in the intentions of our gentile friends during the war. Nevertheless, there was no transportation out of Horodlo on Sundays, so we decided to risk asking Luciowa if we could spend the night in her barn. She agreed.

Before leaving our house, we arranged our beds to look as if we were sleeping in them. Around dusk, we all sneaked out and separately made our way to Luciowa's barn. The next morning, we returned to our house to find that every bed had been pierced with a bayonet.

We immediately hired two wagons, gathered our meager belongings and the five *Sefer Torahs*, and headed to Hrubieszów where we had heard several Jewish survivors had gathered. I was in one wagon with Fishel, Leibel, Chipele, and the five *Sefer Torahs*. The second wagon left after us with two boys, Dovid Berger and a boy named Yankel. The other Jews in our group left separately.

I had gotten to know Yankel when he came to Horodlo after the war. He had received a letter from the Soviet Union informing him that his family had survived the war in Siberia. Although he had lost his wife and a young daughter, his mother, father, sisters, and brothers were all alive. I had helped Yankel pen a letter to his family, telling them that he had also survived.

My wagon arrived safely in Hrubieszów where we waited for our friends. As evening approached, we learned that as the second wagon passed the town of Strzyżów, Dovid and Yankel, were hauled off the wagon and shot in broad daylight while people stood by and silently watched. Imagine the pain and anguish Yankel's family suffered when they returned from the Soviet Union to learn that the Poles had murdered Yankel *after* the war.

Fishel arranged a house for us in Hrubieszów, while Leibel and Chipele found another place to stay. Joining us was Chana

Zuberman, who had shared our house in Horodlo. About a week or two after our arrival in the spring of 1945, four people arrived from Volodymyr: the Boksenboim siblings – two sisters and a brother (whose mother was born in Horodlo) – and a man named Shia Blai who had survived the war with my cousin Yankel Zawidowicz. The Nazis had murdered Shia Blai's wife and all six of his children.

As it turned out, life in Hrubieszów was not safe either. Poles raided Jewish homes at night looking for people to kill. Jews who tried to leave risked being caught on the road and murdered. Once, we found the body of a dead Jewish boy lying in the street and took him to the cemetery for burial.

Our living quarters consisted of a kitchen and one room in which all six of us slept. A Polish family lived on the other side of the house. They had a daughter whose lover was a Soviet officer and when she brought him home to spend the night, her parents objected and threw her out. When we heard what had happened, we jumped at the opportunity to invite this young couple to join us and sleep in our kitchen. In this way, we felt more protected from the Polish bandits. One night, some Poles came knocking at our door with the excuse that they needed to check our passports. To their surprise, the officer jumped out of bed and started shooting through the door, yelling at them, "How dare you ask to check the passport of a Soviet officer!" He threatened to kill them and swore at them in Russian. They quickly vanished, never to return.

Although it was dangerous for Jews to travel to other towns, I had the Christian identity card that Matewka had made for me while I was in hiding. I may not have needed it then, but it came in very handy after the war.

Shia Blai and I decided to leave Hrubieszów. The others were planning to leave too, and we were all concerned about the Torah scrolls that were in our possession. It was impossible for us to keep traveling with them, especially if I was posing as a Christian. Fishel encountered a Jewish man in Hrubieszów who had survived the war with his family in the Soviet Union and he agreed to take the *Sefer*

Torahs from us.[1]

At that time, there were Russian truck drivers who, for a fee, would drive Polish merchants to the city of Lublin to purchase merchandise and bring it back to Hrubieszów to sell in the market. Shia and I posed as merchants and headed to Lublin along with the Poles. On the road, two Polish bandits dressed in Red Army uniforms stopped our truck to inspect our documents. They informed us that they were hunting for Jews. Terrified, I struggled to control my trembling hands as I displayed my false document. Satisfied with my identification card, the marauders turned to search the others. I glanced over at Shia, knowing that he did not have any papers. Paralyzed by the horror that they would determine that Shia was Jewish, I sat motionless and felt my sweat drench my skin and the thumping of my heart against my chest. Just as the bandits were about to search the others, a woman on the truck sitting next to me exclaimed, "You don't have to search us. If there were any Jews among us, we'd kill them ourselves!" The brigands glanced around and did not bother checking the men's passports. Little did that woman know that her brazen comment had saved my Jewish friend.[2]

When we reached Lublin, Shia connected us with a Jewish family with whom we spent the night. The next day we headed to the train station to go to the city of Lodz, almost three hundred kilometers away. So as not to betray our Jewish identities, Shia and

---

[1] Years later, we learned that this man, his family, and the Torah scrolls all made it safely to Israel. I am frustrated that I cannot remember this man's name because I would have sought him out when I visited Israel.

[2] Fifty years later, in 1995, when I was interviewed for a McGill University journal in Montreal, Canada, I discovered that the fake Polish passport I held, identified me as a Ukrainian national. Polish passports stamped with the Trident (the official Ukrainian coat of arms) were issued to Ukrainian nationals living in Poland so that upon review of these passports, the Nazis were able to recognize their Ukrainian collaborators. Had those Soviet bandits been literate, they would have killed me, not for being a Jew, but for being a Ukrainian. (See photo of the Fake Identification Card, Chapter 15, page 106.)

I pretended not to know one another when we traveled together. At the station in Lublin, Shia bought us tickets and we waited separately for the train. The first two trains that arrived were crammed full of people, as were all the trains that followed. It was getting late, and we feared that none of the trains would have space for us. Frustrated that we would never reach our destination, Shia suggested that we climb onto the roof of the train. "Are you crazy? I had not survived the war to die falling off a train!" I exclaimed. So, we waited.

When one of the seemingly jam-packed trains arrived, a Polish soldier suddenly bolted out, and asked me why I was not boarding. When I told him that the train was too crowded to board, he explained that the trains were almost empty inside – the Poles were making the train cars appear full by congregating near the doors, so Jews could not embark. He grabbed my knapsack, took hold of me under my arm, and escorted me onto the empty train. Pointing at Shia Blai, who was sitting at one side of the station, I courageously told the soldier that I had noticed this man who had also been waiting all day for a train. The soldier promptly replied, "We Poles stick together and help each other!" He bounced down the step and helped Shia onto the train. Fearing that any eye contact between Shia and me might raise suspicions, I was quite relieved when Shia chose to sit in another car.

The soldier sat next to me, and I remained anxious and uncomfortable as he flirted with me the entire night. When the time came for him to disembark, he asked for my address. I quickly and shrewdly conjured up a fake address and told him that I was staying on "Zielona Street," which in English translates to Green Street. I stifled a giggle as he promised to visit me that Sunday.

Before the war, Lodz had been home to the second-largest Jewish community in Poland, after Warsaw, and a large group of Jewish survivors was already gathering there. In February 1945, the Provisional Jewish Committee had already been established to help the flood of Jewish refugees flocking to the city.

A few days after coming to Lodz, I met a friend from Horodlo

Freda. Szczecin, 1946.

named Sarah Hecht. Happily, I had particularly good news to report to her – just before leaving Horodlo, I had received a letter from City Hall listing her family as being alive in the Soviet Union. Thrilled with the news and delighted to see me, we stayed in contact and one afternoon, she invited me to go to a movie. Sarah was familiar with Lodz because she had lived there for a few years before the war. The film we saw was only the second movie I had ever seen in my life. Years earlier, I had watched the movie *Titanic* with my elementary school class, but it had been a silent film.

As we were leaving the theater, a group of Polish soldiers accosted some Jews in the street and began beating them with whips. Everyone scattered in all directions, and I lost my friend. I did not know where to run; I had only been in Lodz a couple of days. Then I realized that running would alert the soldiers to the fact that I, too, was Jewish. Instead, I slowly walked around, observing the awful scene. One of the soldiers ran over to me and asked me where I was going. Once again, I used the address that I had given the Polish soldier on the train – Zielona Street. It turned out that my make-believe street was really a street in Lodz! The soldier escorted me out of the tumult, telling me that this was not a place for a "Polish girl," and walked me part way "home."

It did not take me long to realize that even Lodz was no place for Jews. A few of us decided to head to the large, port city of Szczecin – the former German town of Stettin. Since a piece of Poland had been given to Ukraine after the war, Poland was compensated with a few German cities and Szczecin had been one of them. The Poles there were so busy expropriating the Germans of their houses,

Freda's registration card obtained in Szczecin showing her residing at Szwarceukopf 10 Apt. 9 as of August 24, 1945, having previously lived in Horodlo.

they left the Jews alone for a while. Also, when the Soviet Union finally allowed Polish Jewish refugees to be repatriated to Poland in late 1945 and through 1946, they arrived on trains that stopped in both Szczecin and a town called Police,[3] about fifteen kilometers north of Szczecin.

In Szczecin, I found a job working in a grocery store owned by Jews. I was later transferred to Police to work in one of their other stores that included a restaurant. I was still posing as a Polish Catholic girl and had been registered as the owner of the store. In Police, I faced another type of danger – the Soviets and the Poles would frequent the restaurant where I worked and, when they got drunk, there was so much hostility that skirmishes would break out between them. They would shoot wildly at the ceiling and I was the one who had to break them apart.

Polish officers were now returning from England along with the elite from the Ander's Army, an anti-Nazi armed force of Polish and Jewish refugees led by General Wladyslaw Anders. I met many of them in the store. One officer always flirted with me and asked me out on a date. I told him I had a boyfriend in Szczecin with whom I spent my weekends, even though I never left Police. One time, he ran into the store bewildered and upset that Jews were returning to Poland on the trains from the Soviet Union. He could not believe so many Jews had survived. He had been hoping the country would be free of Jews. "Hitler was definitely a murderer," he declared, "but one good thing he did was to exterminate the Jews for us." His unabashed, blatant, antisemitic outcry made my blood curdle and I was so irate that it took everything within me to refrain from responding.

**

The arrival of the Jewish refugees in the cattle trains from the Soviet Union was a horrifying sight. People were shrouded in filthy

---

[3] The Polish town of Police is known as Pölitz in German.

rags; their faces were hollow and grey, and their starvation was evident. Men, women, and children arrived daily on these trains. With each trainload of refugees, I ran to see if my father was among them. I had been anticipating our reunion ever since I forwarded my address to him.

One day an old Jewish man who had just arrived on the train came into the store, took a few zlotys out of his pocket, and asked me to sell him a piece of bread. This was an unusual request since bread was sold by the loaf. Recognizing that he was hungry, I took a loaf of bread, some butter and some cheese, placed it into a bag, and gave it to him. He explained that he did not have the money to pay for the groceries. "Please keep your money and take the food," I insisted.

As he left the store, I heard him tell the others, "There is a Polish girl inside the store who is among the *Chasidei Umas Ha'olam* (Righteous Gentiles)," and displayed the food I had given him. When the others came into the store, I gave them food as well. This time, however, I did not want my kindness and generosity to be attributed to a gentile girl. For the first time since the war's end, I admitted to being Jewish, whispering to them, "*Ich bin a yiddishe tochter mit a yiddishe hartz*" (I am a Jewish girl with a Jewish heart).

That same day, while I was outside resting in front of the store, two Yiddish speaking people walked by me. One was a young man dressed in a soldier's uniform and the other was a woman wearing galoshes tied with string. Without seeing her face, I immediately recognized the woman's voice. She had been one of my neighbors in Horodlo. Her husband, Benzion Handel, had been my brother's rebbe. The man in the soldier's uniform was one of her sons, Yidl. When I asked her if her name was Faiga, she stopped in her tracks, shocked that I knew her. She did not recognize me. I invited her into the store and took her into a back room where I quietly began to speak to her in Yiddish. I asked about her children, mentioning each by name: Moishe, Yidl, Henoch, Ruchel, Sarah, and a sixth child whose name I cannot remember. Her children had all survived in the Soviet Union, but her husband had died digging trenches for

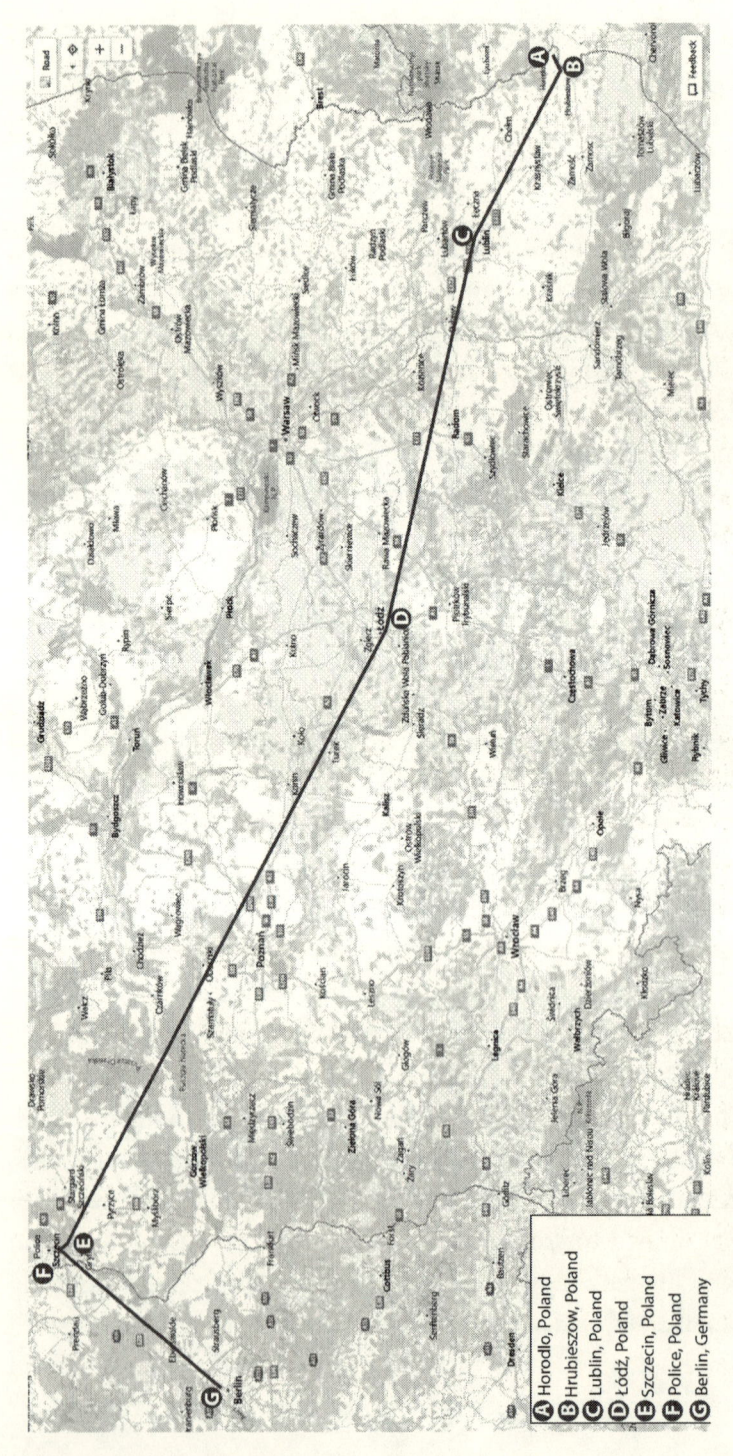

After the war, Horodło proved to be unsafe for Freda and her remaining Jewish friends. This was true for all Polish cities, as Jewish survivors met with antisemitic violence by Polish citizens. This map shows Freda's post-war travels in search of safety.

Ⓐ Horodło, Poland
Ⓑ Hrubieszów, Poland
Ⓒ Lublin, Poland
Ⓓ Łódź, Poland
Ⓔ Szczecin, Poland
Ⓕ Police, Poland
Ⓖ Berlin, Germany

the Soviet army. She still did not know who I was and begged me to tell her.

When I told her that I was Fradl Perelmuter, she was shocked, and could not comprehend how I could be so far from Horodlo. She asked me where my family was and I told her they had been murdered in Sobibor, except for my oldest brother, Moshe Levi Yitzchak, who was murdered in Volodymyr, and my father, whom I was expecting to arrive any day on one of the cattle cars from the Soviet Union. When Faiga and her son left the store, I told them to return in the evening. I felt that I had to help this family. They had nothing.

There were Germans who came to the store to barter clothing for food, but they rarely offered anything I needed. On this day, I posted a sign on my store window saying that I was accepting clothing for a woman, three boys, and three girls. By day's end, I had gathered three large sacks of clothes.

Faiga and her son returned in the evening, and I handed them the sacks of clothing. I accompanied them to their temporary dwelling to meet the rest of their family. I had not seen them in six years. After a bittersweet reunion, I opened the sacks and dressed them from head to toe. As I left, I told them to come back to the store the following day. When they returned, I gave them as much food as they could carry. I knew that the owners were planning to close the store and move to Berlin with other Jewish survivors, and I would be leaving with my father as soon as he arrived. The Handels were so grateful for my charity. I later learned that the Handels eventually settled in Israel.

On the day of the store's closing, the Polish officer who had pursued me came to visit. I knew how precarious my situation was and how foolish I would be to say anything, but I could no longer resist. "You know the girl that you have been flirting with all this time?" I asked. "She is one of those Jews that you wished Hitler had exterminated!!!" I walked away leaving him flushed and speechless.

CHAPTER SEVENTEEN

Is This My Father?

One Sunday in 1946, I encountered two men coming up the stairs in my apartment building in Szczecin just as I was walking down. They were speaking in Yiddish, and I immediately recognized my father's voice. His familiar-looking hand resting on the banister, confirmed that it was indeed my father, but there was nothing else about him that was recognizable. My father was then forty-nine years old but looked like an incredibly old man. He had no teeth, no beard, wore glasses, and was dressed in Soviet-style clothing. When I last saw him in Horodlo at the outbreak of the war, he had been a young, bearded father of five, dressed in Chassidic garb.

Instinctively, I turned and said, "This is my father." For his part, my father did not recognize the German-looking woman with braided, blond hair and modern clothing either. He had last seen me when I was a teenager. Seeing his confusion, I said, "*Ich bin dayn tochter, Fradl*" (I am your daughter, Fradl). Once he realized who I was, we embraced and were overcome with emotion. We could not stop crying, overwhelmed by more longing and loss than most people ever experience. At the same time, there was some awkwardness to the reunion – I wished to embrace the father I remembered from Horodlo. I led him and his friend to my apartment, although my father's friend soon left.

While in the apartment, we shared our wartime experiences. My story came pouring out of me like an onrush of water over a broken dam. I told my father about how quickly life changed after he left and how I worked for the *Kommandant* while we remained in Horodlo. I recounted the story of our neighbor, the Polish policeman, who had whipped Yosele when Yosele volunteered to work in my place. I relayed the grief of our family when we learned that my oldest brother, Moshe Levi Yitzchak, was murdered together with 200 other boys on *Erev Yom Kippur*, 1941. I described to him how I felt when my mother and siblings were driven out of Horodlo, how I thought I would never see them again, and then how elated I was when we were reunited in Uchanie even though it was for such a brief time. I told my father about the last *Pesach* I spent with my mother and siblings in Horodlo, and how my brothers longed for him to lead our *Pesach seder*. I described how delighted and proud Yosele was to become a *Bar Mitzvah*, and how he skirted out of line to retrieve his *tefillin* after the Germans marched us out of Uchanie to Miaczyn. I recounted the last day I saw my mom and siblings and showed him the monogrammed earrings that were pressed into my hand during those final moments of mayhem. I described the hardship of working in Starzeń, my broken arm, and my subsequent escape. Then, I told him about my 21-month solitary confinement beneath the earth, the miraculous birth of Liya, and the indescribable generosity and kindheartedness of Katya and Matewka Budniewski.

My father, in turn, described his survival in a Siberian work camp. He never reached the home of our family members living in Volodymyr. Immediately upon his arrival to the Ukraine, my father was captured by the Soviets and sent to a labor camp in Siberia. Famished and weakened by the little food he received, and often toiling in subzero temperatures, he spent long days felling trees and digging the frozen ground with crude handsaws and pickaxes. He was luckier than those who were forced to mine coal and other minerals, many succumbing to painful lung diseases. Numerous laborers died from exhaustion, starvation, and disease, or were brutally beaten or shot by the camp guards. New prisoners replaced those who died. My father then described how he secretly kept his *tefillin*, which tended to be confiscated by the Soviets to prevent suicides by hanging. Every morning he would crawl under his bunk bed to secretly don his *tefillin*.

It was through our grief and the stories we recounted over several days together, that we slowly began to reconnect and to plan for our future. Our first decision was to travel together to Berlin, where there was a Displaced Persons (DP) camp run by the American Jewish Joint Distribution Center and the United Nations Relief and Rehabilitation Agency (UNRRA).

Freda reunites with her father in Szczecin, 1946.

The trip to Berlin was extremely hazardous. We were not permitted to cross the border into Germany without proper papers, so we had to find another way across. At the time, there was a shortage of gasoline in Berlin and the Soviet soldiers who drove trucks filled with gasoline from Szczecin to Berlin made extra money by smuggling Jews hidden behind the gasoline barrels. Silently crouched behind these supplies, with our knees pulled to our chests, we made this terrifying and nerve-wracking trip across the border to Berlin.

* * *

After Germany's surrender, the country was divided into four zones administered by each of the four Allied forces – the United States, Britain, France, and the Soviet Union. Although Berlin was located entirely within the eastern Soviet sector, the decision was made to similarly divide the city into four administrative zones run by the four Allied forces. The journey to parts of Berlin administered by the Western Allies was made more hazardous because refugees had to first pass through the Soviet-controlled zone.

We arrived safely in the American sector of Berlin at the DP camp called Schlachtensee – also known as the Düppel Center – to find it filled with Jews from all over Europe. Schlachtensee had been a German military base, so it consisted of barracks that had once accommodated the soldiers. Each room had the capacity to house four people on four cots. There was a large dining hall, a kitchen, a swimming pool, a sports arena, a ballroom, and facilities to shower and bathe. A committee, headed by an American named Fishbein, registered the refugees and distributed living accommodations. Food and clothing were plentiful. Cultural activities were established to help the survivors return to some kind of normalcy. There were educational classes for children, a synagogue in which to pray, and a rabbi named Friedman who counseled us and led the men in prayer.

As Jews arrived at the DP camp, the first thing they did was search for members of their family. My father found his cousin Mendel Szulman and his family, who had also survived the war in the Soviet Union. The Szulmans eventually settled in Israel.

As a young 23-year-old girl, I longed for the social life I had for years been deprived of. I felt fortunate to make new friends in Schlachtensee. We all shared the unfortunate common bond of having lost friends and family and told each other stories of how we had survived the war. My father and I befriended a family named Flescher, who lived in the barracks adjacent to ours. The family consisted of two sisters and three brothers – Esther, Ucia, Moishe, Hersh, and Buma. Later, one of their cousins named Yisroel (Srulek) Schwechter arrived in Berlin and joined them. Esther, the oldest girl, took over running the household, substituting for their mother. It was always fun to be around the Fleschers, especially when Srulek, who was on the soccer team, played ball.

I occasionally left the camp to go with friends to the opera and operettas, or to plays and movies. We toured Berlin, even though much of it had been destroyed. During that time, I saw *Tosca*, *Carmen*, and *The Lustike Vidke* (The Merry Widow), to name a few. I still have many of the playbills from these shows.

Every Saturday night, there was always something happening in the camp. There was a dance hall, where boys and girls could socialize. There were movies, sporting events, and other gatherings. Various Jewish organizations sprouted in the DP camp and there was always plenty of activity.

After the war, the Germans were fearful that the Jews would take revenge against them. Some of them were guilty of having committed atrocities and were scared they would be identified. Seeing Jews in Berlin after what they had done to us made them very anxious. It was empowering to see the Germans transformed from hardened, bloody murderers to nervous, feeble, powerless, and weak individuals. In these new circumstances, the panicky, obsequious, and hypocritical Germans did everything they could to ingratiate themselves to the surviving Jews.

Once, our group decided to attend the State Berlin opera, which was situated in the Soviet zone. This was long before the wall was built – there were no physical divisions between the four zones in Berlin. We took a train into the Soviet sector and luckily no one checked our documents. When we entered the opera house, the unctuous German manager, recognizing that we were Jewish, approached us with great flourish and courtesy. He went out of his way to show us respect and asked us where we wanted to sit, even though we had no tickets.

"Hitler's *Loge!*" one of the boys screamed out.

"*Jawohl, jawohl, meine Damen und Herren*" (Certainly, certainly, ladies and gentlemen). "Follow me," he continued, and led us to the most luxurious red plush seating in the opera house. He even provided us with binoculars. There were many Germans present at the opera and we created quite a spectacle as Jews sitting in Hitler's seats.

128 A SOUL BENEATH THE EARTH

Playbills from the operas, movies, and plays that Freda attended while living in the DP camp in Berlin, 1946-1948.

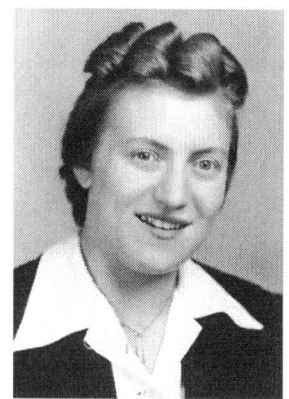

Freda. Berlin, 1947.

Freda, left, and a friend in the Schlachtensee DP camp. Berlin, 1947.

*Freda and her father,
Nosson Nuta Perelmutter.
Berlin, circa 1947.*

*Freda, top right, with friends in
Schlachtensee. Berlin, 1947.*

Is This My Father?

Freda, top left with other Holocaust survivors in the Schlachtesee DP camp. Berlin, 1947.

Freda's father, Nuta, first person on left, in the Schlachtensee DP camp. Berlin, 1947.

Freda celebrates the Jewish New Year in the Schlachtensee DP camp. Berlin, 1947.

Freda. Berlin, 1948.

Throughout the war and hiding in the pit, Freda was determined to keep her long, beautiful hair...

"I cleaned my hair by scrubbing my scalp with a wet cloth and putting about one quarter of a teaspoon of kerosene into my hair, to keep it from tangling and to prevent lice. Then I braided my hair and wrapped the braids around my head to keep it clean. I wore a little kerchief to protect my hair from debris falling from the hay."

CHAPTER EIGHTEEN

A New Life in Canada

My father contacted his brother, Baruch Perelmuter, who had immigrated to Canada before the war with his wife, Toba, and their baby boy. Baruch attempted to bring us to Canada right away, but this was not an easy task. Canada was not eager to welcome Jews, as Canadian historians, Irving Abella and Harold Troper, documented in their book, *None is Too Many: Canada and the Jews of Europe, 1933-1948*.

It took us two years to finally receive our visas to enter Canada. I was 25 years old when we arrived in Montreal, Quebec in September 1948, after a miserable two-week trip on a cargo ship. I was seasick the entire time and the food on the ship was inedible. There was not even a glass of milk to be had; the small supply of milk on the ship was reserved for the infants. Thankfully, Bronya

Uncle Benny (Baruch) and Aunt Toba with their first grandson. Montreal, Canada.

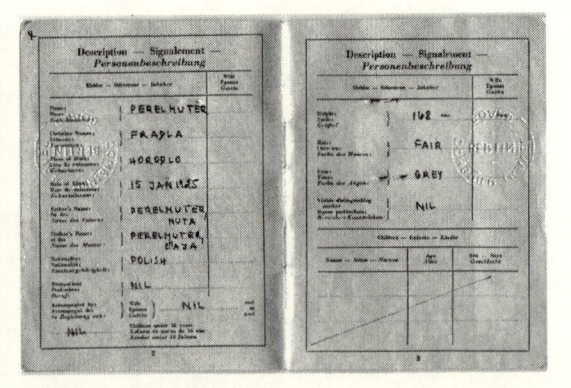

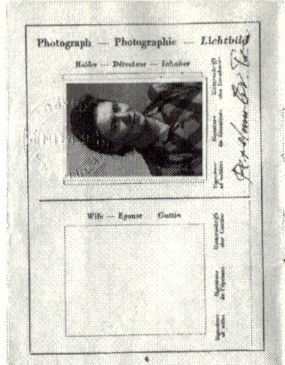

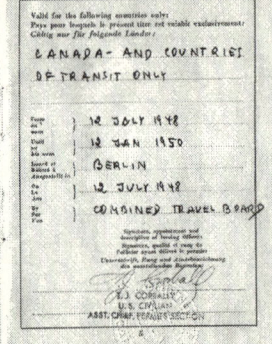

Freda's temporary travel document (issued by the German government in 1948 in lieu of a passport) for travel from Germany to Canada.

Kramer, who was from Chelm, my father's hometown, shared her baby's milk with me.

I had only been in Canada for one week when I collapsed and landed in Montreal's Jewish General Hospital with pneumonia. While I was there, I underwent thyroid surgery. My thyroid had become goitrous due to iodine deficiency forcing me to spend three months in the hospital. My poor, grieving father had to take care of his only remaining child while working at a candy factory making $16 a week and trying to adjust to life in a new country. After recovering from my illness, I soon found work as a clothing finisher earning $12 a week.

We rented a basement room with a small kitchen on Colonial Street, where many Jews lived at that time. The basement had to be heated with wood and there was no hot water. There was no shower or bath – our bathroom consisted of a toilet that had been squeezed into a small closet – and we had an icebox instead of a refrigerator. When I would return home from work, it was so cold in our basement that I cooked our meals wearing my overcoat.

Despite these difficult circumstances, we did not complain. Nothing could compare to what I had experienced under Nazi occupation and what my father had suffered in Siberia. At least we slept in peace, not worrying that someone would drag us out in the middle of the night and murder us. We lived with hope that times would get better.

Adjusting to a new country was not easy. Language and customs were different – we spoke neither English nor French – everything was completely new. We met other survivors. We affectionately called each other the *"greeners"* or *"greenhorns,"* a term used to describe our status as novice, inexperienced newcomers. We had little money and little schooling as our lives had been upended by the war. Furthermore, our hearts were battered and broken from our indescribable suffering and loss.

We did not allow ourselves to focus on all that we lost and all our misfortunes because *we were the lucky ones!* We were in a new land, and we had to survive! Life was hard but we felt safe in our new country. We were grateful to *Hashem* that He had brought us out of the ashes to begin life anew in Canada. My evenings were spent attending English classes at Baron Byng High School on St. Urban Street in Montreal, close to where I lived. Baron Byng had a rich history of Jewish life that began in the 1920s, when it was first built, reached a Jewish student population of 99% by 1938, and ended in the 1960s when the Jewish immigrants

Nosson Nuta Perelmuter, Montreal, 1950.

living in that neighborhood moved elsewhere and were replaced by Greek immigrants. The famous author, Mordechai Richler, and the renowned oncologist, Dr. Phil Gold, were both graduates of Baron Byng High School.

I knew that I had to master the English language to adjust to my new country, so I studied and practiced as much as possible. Just as I had taught myself Russian while hiding in the pit from the Germans, I was determined to learn English. I bought a Polish-English dictionary and began writing lists of letters, words, and sentences. I had a friend who wrote to me in English. I studied those letters when I received them, then used those words in my answers. I still have some of those letters and the drafts of my replies.

I now had a group of friends – all Holocaust survivors – with whom I would socialize. On weekends, we would gather at the foot of Mount Royal, the mountain located in the center of the city, from which Montreal derives its name. Occasionally we would all go to the movies or attend the various clubs, socials and newcomer dances sponsored especially for us by the Young Men-Young Women Hebrew Association (YM-YWHA). In addition, we would avail ourselves of the resources at the nearby Jewish Public Library (JPL), which offered courses on learning English, Jewish and world history, Yiddish literature, and Canada. Both the YM-YWHA and the JPL served an integral role in helping us move beyond our traumatic past and rebuild our social lives.

This was my life for the next four years – working hard to make ends meet, learning English, cooking, caring for my father, and socializing and dating on the weekends. I was slowly adjusting to my new country that was providing me with my new freedom. Yet not a day passed that I did not cry about the loss of my mother, my brothers, my baby sister, my aunts, my uncles, my cousins, and my grandparents.

CHAPTER NINETEEN

Mendel and Family

My life changed when I met my husband. In 1951, married friends of mine from Toronto wrote to tell me that a man by the name of Menachem Mendel Schipper, also a Holocaust survivor, was coming to send regards from them. This was their attempt at making a *shidduch*, or match, for me. They explained that Mendel was coming to Montreal with his Polish friend, Karol Mozdzen, who had moved to Canada before the war and was instrumental in bringing Mendel to Winnipeg. The Mozdzen family were Christian neighbors of Mendel in Poland. Near the end of the war, Mendel and his brother were hidden in the attic of Karol's mother. It was only after Mendel's arrival in Winnipeg that Karol discovered that it was his own mother who had hidden Mendel and his older brother, Hersh.

I was both excited and nervous when they knocked at my door. I mistakenly thought that Mendel was the Polish man because of his piercing blue eyes and blond hair. I began to speak to Mendel in Polish and to his Polish friend in Yiddish. Mendel found this quite amusing and cracked a huge smile as he corrected me. I think I fell in love immediately.

I learned that Mendel and his brother, Hersh, grew up in the southeastern Polish village of Wolica, in Przeworsk County,

Mendel and his family. Poland, 1938.

Back row standing left to right: Mendel, his brother, Hersh, Nechemia Engelberg, (cousin) Tsila and Leibish Engelberg (cousin), Naftali Engelberg (cousin).

Front row seated left to right: Sarah Engelberg Schipper (mother of Mendel and Hersh), Chaya Ruchel and Avraham Todress Engelberg, (Mendel's maternal grandparents), Faige and Aaron Engelberg (Mendel's aunt and uncle).

Children: Tsila and Leibish's daughters, Miriam (left) Sally (right).

Tsila and Leibish and their three daughters (daughter, Lola, is not pictured here) and other family members survived the war with the help of a Polish family who hid them in their attic.

approximately 20 miles east of the regional capital, Rzeszow. (Mendel's family tree can be found in Appendix IV, pages 10 and 11.)

During the war, Mendel's parents, Sarah, the daughter of Avraham Engelberg, and Chaim, the son of Tzvi Hersh Schipper, went into hiding with their sons. One day, as the Germans descended into the woods, Mendel's parents were discovered. As Mendel and Hersh lay hidden in nearby bushes, they witnessed their parents being taken to the cemetery and heard the two gunshots that killed them both.

Mendel and Hersh survived the war by daring to escape from the Pustkow labor camp infirmary and hiding in the woods for several years. There were times that the two brothers slept under the snow. They managed to survive by forming liaisons with the Polish underground, procuring food, lodging, and firearms, and drawing upon their strength and determination to defend themselves as necessary when danger lurked too near. After the war ended, their liberation did not bring immediate relief as they miraculously survived a pogrom in the town of Rzeszow on June 12, 1945, where the Poles killed 15 Jews.

After his visit to Montreal, Mendel returned to Toronto, and we began writing letters to each other. I still have the stack of these letters from all those years ago. My Canadian cousins laughed at me, warning me that to wait for a man who lives in Toronto, whom I had only met on one occasion, was foolish. After all, when would I see him again? How could this relationship survive the long distance?

Six months later, Mendel came to visit and on that second encounter, we got engaged.

Freda and Mendel exchange photos in April and May of 1951.

On March 2, 1952, Mendel and I married. The marriage and my wedding ceremony were both extremely exciting and bittersweet. I

Freda and Mendel. Montreal, 1952.

was thrilled to be marrying the man I loved so very much, and happy to be able to collect the pieces of my shattered past and look to the future. But I also remember the deep sadness I felt at not having my dear mother walk me down the aisle or my siblings to smile at my good fortune. I have felt this way for all my life's milestones. Mendel understood this sadness in me as he felt the same, having also lost his family to the murdering Germans. His only brother, Hersh, with whom Mendel had survived the war, was stuck in Munich, unable to obtain papers to come to Canada.

I did not care that my wedding dress was borrowed, and I took great pride in the fact that my father and I were able to afford a small wedding replete with good food and drink.

After we married, Mendel moved into the wretched, one room apartment that I shared with my father on Colonial Street in the St. Lawrence neighborhood of Montreal. During the nights, we hung a sheet in the center of the room separating our bed from my father's. This was our privacy! By day, this cold, damp chamber served as our living room and kitchen.

*Freda and Mendel at their wedding.
March 2, 1952. Montreal, Canada.*

*Freda and Mendel attend
a friend's wedding.
Montreal, 1953.*

* * *

The way Mendel landed his first job in Montreal accurately reflects the way we, as survivors, viewed and conducted our lives. We were driven by both the need to survive and the determination to strive for a better life.

Mendel found an ad in a newspaper indicating that Canadair, a civil and military aircraft manufacturer, was searching for a mechanic to assemble engine parts. Experience was required. Of course, Mendel had no experience, but he did have the gumption and the "nothing to lose" attitude to apply for the job. During the interview, when my husband was asked about experience, he answered "I do not have any experience whatsoever, but I am smart, honest, trustworthy, and I learn quickly. I volunteer to work without pay for a month, during which time I will learn everything I need to know to do this job. I promise to become your best worker and that you will not be disappointed. If after a month you will be dissatisfied with my performance, I will look for work elsewhere. However, if my work is satisfactory, I will expect to be hired for the job."

Over the course of this period, Mendel proved his capabilities. And so, Mendel secured his first job in Montreal, working long nights to earn time-and-a-half wage. At the same time, he began to perfect his English and began to learn French, as both languages were the official languages in Quebec, and both were needed for any future higher level of employment.

***

When I became pregnant, we knew that it was impossible to raise a child in the conditions in which we were living, so we had

Freda and Mendel Schipper with their firstborn child, Chaim Moshe. Freda was pregnant with Sandy at the time this photo was taken.

to move. The three of us moved to a walk-up apartment on Van Horne Street in the Outremont neighborhood in Montreal. To our delight, our son, Hyman Morris (Chaim Moshe), named for Mendel's father, Chaim, and my brother, Moshe Levi Yitzchak, was born on April 11, 1954 (8th of Nisan, 5714) at Montreal's Jewish General Hospital. No one could have prepared us for this kind of joy! To bring a healthy child into the world after we had suffered such atrocities was miraculous.

Nuta Perelmuter and Chaim. "The first time my father really smiled after the war was when his first grandchild was born."

Hitler was unsuccessful in killing off my family tree. My father, for the first time since the war, was genuinely happy.

* * *

After a few years of working at Canadair, Mendel left to become a shareholder at a department store called the Canadian Outfitting Company on St. Lawrence Blvd.[1] Although the hours were long and grueling, life became a little easier. I was now a stay-at-home mom raising our beautiful son.

On December 29, 1956 (the 25th of Tevet, 5717), I once again returned to the Jewish General Hospital and gave birth to our daughter, Irene Sandra (Chaya Sarah), who we named after both our mothers. Known today as Sandy, our beautiful daughter arrived into the world in the middle of a blizzard. Nothing could deter this

---

[1] The department store offered credit and payment terms to each shareholder's proprietary customer base in a pre-credit card era. The shareholders would be responsible for meeting clients by appointment at the store to promote sales and for visiting their clients to collect payments.

blissful event in our lives!

My life became busy raising our two children. Chaim began school, and because I did not drive, getting him there and back by bus or on foot in Montreal winters was hectic. Luckily, my father became a tremendous support system, lending assistance whenever needed.

On September 27, 1960 (the 6th of Tishrei, 5721), I was delighted to return to the Jewish General Hospital where *Hashem* blessed us once again with the birth of another baby boy, Saul (Yisroel). We named him after my paternal grandfather.

Freda and Mendel with Freda's father, Nuta (seated) holding Sandy, and 3-year-old Chaim.

Despite the happiness of my family life in Montreal, I have always been haunted by the loss of my family in Poland. I would never be able to have enough children to provide a namesake for all the lost souls in my family. I secretly wept for the grandparents, aunts, uncles, and cousins; those whom my children would never know.

We lived in our apartment on Van Horne St. for nine years. During those early years, we summered with other Holocaust survivors in a bungalow colony in Val Morin, a bucolic town located in the Laurentian Mountains about an hour's drive north

Freda with her children, Chaim (left), Sandy (right), and Saul (center). October 1962.

of Montreal. As it was with many of the men in our social circle, Mendel and my father worked in the city during the weekdays and joined us in the country for weekends. Our children had many friends and enjoyed playing outdoors. Chaim, my oldest, forged a lifelong interest in nature. The magnificent scenery, the fresh mountain air, the clear-water lakes, and the friendships I honed, made summer a time I would look forward to.

In 1962, we bought a house on Kincourt Ave in the town of Côte St. Luc, a suburb of Montreal, where I have lived for over fifty years. Our wonderful street was populated with other Holocaust survivors. Soon, they became our extended family, and we became theirs.

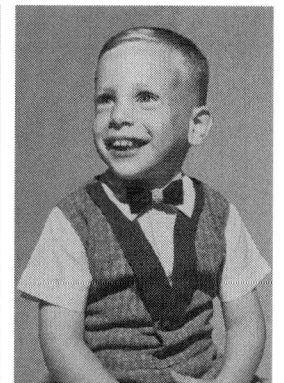

Left to right: Hyman, Sandy and Saul, circa 1963.

Now that we had our family and were living comfortably, our new goal was to give our three children everything we did not have. We invested all our energies into raising our children to become solid, honest human beings. We wanted them to be healthy, safe, and successful. Despite how expensive Jewish parochial school tuition was for us in the beginning, we did everything to ensure that our children received the best education possible. We encouraged them to study, with the hope that they would become professionals. We felt that an education and a profession could never be lost or stolen. So great was our desire for them to have a better, easier life, we scrimped and saved for them to have more.

Our son, Chaim, became a *Bar Mitzvah* in April 1967, and did a beautiful job reading his *parsha* (the Torah portion) and *haftorah*.[2] In addition to the customary *Shabbos kiddush* (a post Sabbath service, celebratory meal), we celebrated with a big, Sunday evening affair. How proud we were of him and how joyous we felt to have witnessed this milestone. I felt truly blessed. Despite my exuberance at being in a place in my life that

Chaim, on the occasion of his Bar Mitzvah. Montreal, 1967

I could never have imagined in the dark days of my hiding in the pit, my excitement was tempered by the memory of my dear brother, Mordechai Yosef Elazar (Yosele), and how he had clandestinely prepared for his *Bar Mitzvah* during the war in 1942. These sentiments

*Saul's Bar Mitzvah celebration. Montreal, 1973.
Left to right: Zeide Nuta, Chaim, Saul, Freda, Sandy, and Mendel*

---

[2] A *haftorah* is a short reading from the Prophets that follows the Torah reading.

returned when we celebrated a second *Bar Mitzvah* with our son, Saul, in 1973.

In 1968, Mendel left the Canadian Outfitting Company to partner with three other Holocaust survivors and began a real estate construction company called Adiro Construction. Although I had full faith in my husband's ability to succeed, I was nonetheless apprehensive. We now owned our own home and had three school-aged children. Mendel had done well in the department store, and we were living comfortably. Mendel was ambitious and determined to augment the security of our family. Eventually, with tremendous drive and resolution, he and his partners built a successful company. I have always been grateful to *Hashem* for what we have.

* * *

We have always been engaged in Jewish community life. Since moving to Côte St. Luc, we became active members of the Beth Zion Synagogue, our beloved *shul*, which we attended regularly with my father. Involved with much of our *shul* activity, Mendel proudly served on the Board of Directors for many years. Working in construction, he played a pivotal role in building the town's *mikvah* (ritual bath) by providing them with an architect and workers at considerable savings.

Freda and Mendel at a Torah dedication at their beloved shul, the Beth Zion Synagogue. Montreal.

As for me, I relished participating in the Beth Zion women's group to study the weekly *parsha*, the Torah portion read on the Sabbath. I was particularly delighted when the *shul* honored me as *Eishet Chayil* (A Woman of Valor) on October 22, 2000. I joined the *Emunah* organization and, with my knowledge of *Chumash* and Jewish studies, I was elected to give the *Dvar Torah* (sermon) to my *Emunah* group monthly, which I did for many years. In addition, we often traveled to Israel, with the *Emunah* organization, with our synagogue, and privately, always stopping in Germany to visit Mendel's brother, Hersh, who was unable to immigrate to Canada after the war.

We were involved in various Jewish causes and always gave *tzedakah* (charity) with an open heart. I could never turn away anyone in need, remembering the hunger and other hardships I had endured during and after the war.

A plaque honoring Freda as Eishet Chayil (A Woman of Valor). October, 2000.

***

My father lived with us for the rest of his life. He died on August 5, 1979 (12th of Av, 5739), at the age of 82. Over 500 people attended his funeral. We had many friends and family in attendance because of our deep involvement with our synagogue and community. This large turnout was even more remarkable because, as per his wishes, his funeral was held within hours of his death.[3] Unabashed, I cried uncontrollably at his burial, as the

Freda's father, Nosson Nuta Perelmuter. Montreal, 1973.

---

[3] According to Jewish tradition, the soul begins its ascent to heaven once the body is buried. It is therefore customary to bury the dead as soon as possible.

memory of family loss once again creeped into my soul. I could not fathom the loss of my *tatte*, my father, the only grandparent to my children. He was the sole member of my immediate family who had accompanied me into my new life – my life after the war. Despite having suffered such inconceivable grief at the loss of his entire family, save for me, he never lost his faith in God. He lived a pious life and instilled in my children the love of Torah and *mitzvos* (good deeds). Over the years, Mendel, the children, and I, formed a profound connection with my father, punctuated by attentiveness and reverence. Seeing Mendel, Chaim, Sandy, and Saul so emotionally distraught over his loss, further heightened the pain of my sadness and grief.

But as I had unfortunately come to know, life continues after grief, and with the support of Mendel and our children, I forged on – with my father joining my other family members living in my heart. I look back at the time he was with us, and I am profoundly grateful for those wonderful years.

I am proud of my three children and their accomplishments. My eldest son, Chaim, earned his M.D. and Ph.D. degrees from McGill University. He is a tenured professor of medicine at the university and works as a neurologist at the Jewish General Hospital in Montreal where he directs a research laboratory for neurodegenerative diseases in the hospital's Lady Davis Institute. He is married to Ruchie or Rachel (Ruchel Leah) Rubinstein, the daughter of Clara (Kayla) Zehnwirth and Avraham Akiva Rubinstein (Radziner Chassidim who also miraculously survived the war). Rachel Rubinstein is a successful dermatologist in Montreal. They have two boys, Tani (Natan Yehoshua) and Dovid (Alter Dovid).

My daughter, Sandy, earned her Bachelor of Science degree in Occupational Therapy from McGill University. She was Director of Occupational Therapy at Franklin Hospital Medical Center on Long Island, New York, where she currently lives with her husband, George (Yaakov) Wolberg, and their son, Jeffrey Nathan (Shalom Natan). George is a tenured professor of Computer Science at the

City College of New York and co-founder of several technology companies. George is the son of Saul (Shalom) Wolberg and Elaine (Yenta) Felder, daughter of Yaakov and Sima Kornreich Felder. George's mother, aunt, and grandparents left Sanok, Poland, for Argentina in 1938.

Saul, my youngest son, earned his Bachelor of Commerce degree from McGill University, an MBA from Concordia, an L.L.B. in Common Law from Dalhousie University in Halifax, and an L.L.B. in Civil Law from l'Université de Montréal. He is married to Stephanie Kapusta, a social worker, the daughter of Miriam Cherow and Dr. Morton Kapusta. They have four daughters: Zoe Rachel (Ziesl Tsirel), Sarah Leah (Sarah Leah), Mayah Natania (Chaya Natania), and Danielle Hannah (Ariel Chana).

Family portrait at Chaim and Ruchie's wedding. New York, 1994.
Seated: Sandy and Chaim
Standing, left to right: Stephanie, Saul, Mendel, Ruchie and Freda.

Saul and Stephanie's wedding. Montreal, 1994.
From left to right: Sandy, Mendel, Stephanie and Saul, Freda, and Chaim.

Celebrating Sandy and George's wedding. New York, 1998.
Seated, left to right: Stephanie, Mendel, Zoe, Tani, Freda and Ruchie.
Standing, left to right: Saul, Sandy and George, Chaim and Dovid.

Freda and Mendel with their children and grandchildren. Montreal, 2005.

Top row from left: Stephanie, holding Danielle, Saul, Freda, Mendel, Ruchie, and Chaim. Bottom from left: Sarah, Zoe, Mayah, Tani, Dovid, Jeffrey, Sandy, and George.

Mendel (center) with daughter, Sandy (left) and grandson, Jeffrey (right). Montreal, 2007.

*At granddaughter, Zoe's Bat Mitzvah.
Freda (right) and Mendel (center) with, from left to right, their children,
Chaim, Saul, and Sandy. Montreal, 2007.*

Our family at Zoe's Bat Mitzvah. Montreal, 2007.

***

It has been my life's mission to educate people about the Holocaust to ensure that future generations never forget the evil that befell us. I have lectured at schools and synagogues and told my story to anyone willing to listen. I have written articles in newspapers and contacted authors whenever I found inaccuracies in their publications. I gave a four-hour testimony to McGill University in 1993, as part of a testimonial project spearheaded by Yehudi Lindeman. In the fall of 1995, I was interviewed for an article about Mr. Lindeman's work that appeared in the McGill University Quarterly Journal. Although these interviews were emotionally and psychologically draining for me, I was buoyed by the importance I have always felt of documenting the horrors of the Holocaust.

We built a good, comfortable life in Montreal, surrounded by family and friends. However, the scars from my wartime experience left an indelible mark on me. I suffer from terrible nightmares, severe claustrophobia, asthma, and chronic bronchitis. Despite my happiness in seeing my children and grandchildren grow, there has never been a day that I have not thought about my mother, my three brothers, my little sister, and the nearly one hundred family members who perished in the Holocaust.

I never returned to Poland. Nothing was left there for me but horrible memories and the scattered remains of my family and friends. Before the war, 3.5 million Jews lived in Poland. Approximately 350,000 managed to survive, most escaping to the Soviet Union, with smaller numbers reaching Sweden, Switzerland, the United States, Canada, Palestine and to whatever countries would admit them. Fewer than 100,000 survivors remained in Poland after the war.

You might be wondering what happened to my saviors. I never saw the Budniewskis again after they left Poland for the Ukraine in 1944, although I kept in touch with them my entire life. When I came to Canada, we exchanged letters and I sent them whatever parcels of clothing I could collect. Later, I used my Russian skills to correspond with their two children, Liya and her younger brother, Galik, who was born after the war and passed away on July 6, 2009 at the age of 61. I have kept in touch with Liya for 68 years and feel privileged to assist her in any way I can.

Matewka died on November 18, 1968, just weeks before his 59th birthday. Katya outlived him, passing away at the age of 73 on October 23, 1983. Neither lived to receive recognition as "Righteous Among the Nations." I sent my story to Yad Vashem and, in 1997, they were posthumously awarded the title and their names were added to the Righteous Honor Wall.[4] Their daughter, Liya, received the award on their behalf.

Why did they put their lives at risk to save me, especially when so few others did? I do not know. I will never comprehend the immensity of their heroism, selflessness, and generosity.

The Germans failed to completely eradicate my past, my family, and my pedigree. Thanks to the Budniewskis, my three children and seven grandchildren continue to nourish my family tree, which is now thriving. They embody the ideals of my ancestors and are a testament to my enduring legacy.

---

[4] The Yad Vashem database records their names as Matvey & Yekaterina Budnevsky.

YAD VASHEM יד ושם

The Holocaust Martyrs and Heroes' Remembrance Authority   רשות הזיכרון לשואה ולגבורה

Jerusalem, 31 March 1997

Mrs. Freda SCHIPPER Shipper
5711 Kincourt Ave.
Quebec
Montreal H4W 1Y7
Canada

Ref: BUDNEVSKI MATVEI & KATERINA - Ukraine (7506)

We are pleased to announce that the above persons were awarded the title of "Righteous Among the Nations," for help rendered to Jewish persons during the period of the Holocaust.

A medal and certificate of honor will be mailed to the Israeli embassy in Kiev, Ukraine, which will organize a ceremony in their honor. Their names will also soon be added on the Righteous Honor Wall at Yad Vashem.

Copies of this letter are being mailed to the honorees, to persons who have submitted testimonies, and other interested parties.

Dr. Mordecai Paldiel
Director, Dept. for the Righteous

cc: Miss Lia Budnevska - Ukraine
Mr. G. Budnevski - Ukraine
Mr. Tzvi Magen - Embassy of Israel, Kiev, Ukraine

1/M.P./D.W./

Letter from Yad Vashem to Freda awarding Matvei (Matewka) and Katerina (Katya) Budnevski (Budniewski) the honor title "Righteous Among the Nations".

Mendel and Family 157

The Righteous Among the Nations medal (both sides) awarded posthumously to Matewka and Katya.

Righteous Among the Nations Certificate

Matewka Budniewski

Matewka and his family. Left to right (rear): Matewka's sister, Hoinia Cherwinska; Matewka and Katya (Mielech) Budniewksi; Matewka's brother, Wasil Budniewski. Seated: Katerina Budniewskaya (Matewka and Wasil's mother). Standing with her arm around her grandmother: Wasil's daughter, Didi Budniewska. Ukraine.

Freda's saviors, Matewka and Katya Budniewski, and their children, Liya and Galik. Ukraine, 1949.

Matewka Budniewski and his children, Galik (left) and Liya (right). Ukraine, 1952.

Liya Budniewska, 1960.

Liya and her son, Matvey (Mitja). Ukraine, 1989.

Galik and his wife, Lidija, with their two children, Liudmila (left) and Anton (right). Volodymyr-Volynsky, Ukraine, 1985.

Below and Next Page:
One of the many, beautifully handwritten letters from Liya during our lifelong correspondences.

сну подобно. Утешаю себя мыслью, что и я рано или поздно буду вместе с отцом. Маме труднее всего. Она пока сама осталась. Плачет, бедная. Галик крепится — он мужчина.

Постараемся быть верными тетиному доброму совету — держаться вместе. Нам с Галиком осталось ещё по 1,5 года учиться. После окончания постараемся попасть на работу домой. Жаль только, что это время маме придется быть одной. Дома мы решили продолжать учебу. Папка так радовался, что мы учимся. Будем приезжать на каникулы. Галику со Львова в 2 раза ближе, чем мне, домой, поэтому он в сезон раза 3-4 будет наведываться и помогать маме. На этом мы пока остановились, потому что бросать институт жалко.

Петю Фрадлю интересовал брат папы, который все время жил в СССР — он умер в 1935 году. И вообще с нашей большой родни осталась одна тетя Аня, сын тети Ани умер в 1948 году, но у тети Ани после него есть внучка. После дяди Вали осталась лишь жена. После дяди Миши остался сын, у него 2 дочери.

На этом кончаю. Будьте все здоровы и счастливы.

Мама Вам допишет от себя в следующем письме (так сама сказала). Целуем Вас крепко крепко
Ваши Будневские
Низкий поклон и пожелания всего лучшего п. Перельмутеру.
Целую еще раз Ляля

PART TWO
Memories of My Mother

by
Sandy Schipper Wolberg

CHAPTER TWENTY

Panic Strikes at EXPO 67

I was ten years old when Montreal hosted the World's Fair, EXPO 67.

Many of the guests who stayed with us while attending the World's Fair regaled us with thrilling stories of what they saw at the fair – plays in open air theaters, costumed dancers on stages, marching bands and exhibits that fueled their curiosity and stirred their imagination.

When my dad announced that we were going to the fair, we piled into the car ready for the day's adventure.

We entered the fairgrounds and felt we stepped into a wonderland. Above us, flags from different countries flapped in the wind. Pavilions built in different architectural styles rose before us like buildings in science fiction books – one shaped like a dome, another a tent, a third metal tubes.

There were people everywhere and everyone was having fun.

One of our first stops was the Western Canada Pavilion, a cone-shaped building virtually without walls, constructed with natural materials from that region. It was situated close to the mini-rail station.

We got in line behind hundreds of people who were shifting their weight from one foot to the other, looking at their watches, fanning themselves with pamphlets and craning their necks to see if they could spot the entrance.

Two and a half hours later, we were close to the front. A guide was letting in groups of about 30 people at a time and directing them to go through a rickety door into what looked like an elevator.

"We will be descending (a virtual) 3,000 feet underground in a mine cage into a tunnel where mining equipment will be displayed," he explained.

When my mother heard the word "underground," her face turned red.

"Ich gay nisht!" (I'm not going!) she shrieked, raising her hands to her cheeks, her lips trembling.

"Fradl," my father reached for her arm, "calm down, it's just an elevator, you will be okay."

But my mom stood motionless, transfixed.

"Mommy." I pleaded, "you'll be with us, we'll all be there together. It will be okay."

She searched our faces but did not recognize us.

"I'm not going," she said shrilly, whirling around and elbowing her way against the crowd, looking for the fastest way out. People who noticed the terror in her eyes cleared the path to let her through, but those looking elsewhere were pushed aside.

I watched my mother disappear into the crowd. Back then, I knew enough about my mother's war experiences to understand what had scared her.

The word "underground," must have triggered flashbacks that thrust her into her past, bombarding her with memories of lying helpless in the pit, alone and terrified, not knowing if she was dead or alive.

The guide motioned us to come forward and we boarded the mine cage. Throughout the exhibit we learned about Western Canada's natural resources. We strolled through forests, prairies and mountain slopes and observed climate changes.

We exited the exhibit and stepped outside. Shading our eyes, we scanned the area to find my mother. Sitting on a bench in the shade, she saw us, smiled, and waved. My brothers and I raced toward her, talking over one another reporting what we learned.

She listened, nodding to each one of us. She was back to being herself.

My father held open a map to figure out where to go next and pointed to another pavilion nearby. We headed toward the building and continued our day as if nothing happened.

CHAPTER TWENTY-ONE

My Yiddishe Momme

The only sound you could hear in my house was running water. It was past 11pm and my mother was washing dishes, having just finished serving dinner to my father, who came home late from work. She had already tidied up the house, hung coats in the closet, placed shoes in the shoe rack.

Outside the wind howled, the swirling snow blanketed Cote Saint Luc, the Montreal suburb we lived in among other Holocaust survivors.

I was still up, snuggling under my big, thick European comforter, reading a book before going to sleep. I shuffled toward the kitchen to get a drink of water and say goodnight to my mother.

But something was different. Along with the swooshing sound of water splashing, I heard a familiar melancholic melody – a song I readily recognized as *My Yiddishe Momme*.

A Yiddishe momme, es gibt nisht besser oyf der velt
A Yiddishe momme, oy vey vi biter ven zi felt
Vi shayn in lichtig iz in hoyz ven di momme iz do
Vi troyerig finster vert ven Got nemt ir oyf Olam Habo.

A Yiddishe momme, there is nothing better in this world

A Yiddishe momme, oy vey how bitter it is when she is gone

How beautiful and radiant is the house when the momme is here

How sad and dark it becomes when God takes her into the World to Come

My mother's voice was low, barely above a whisper. My heart skipped a beat and I felt that familiar pang in my gut whenever my mother drifted into the dark moments of her past.

I turned into the kitchen and found my mother crouched over the sink, leaning on her elbows, holding a plate under the faucet, the water cascading over her soft hands.

"Oh mommy," I cried out, unable to hold back the tears.

My mother, just noticing my presence, turned around, her mournful eyes telling the tale of a thousand deaths, of cattle car doors slamming shut, of Jews huddling together on death marches.

"I lost my dear mother and little sister," she cried in a heavily accented, crackling voice, "my brothers, my family…" Her voice trailed off, too weak to name all the loved ones who perished during the war.

Although I heard my mother's war stories hundreds of times, I felt overwhelmed with emotion.

I reached out to hug her and put my arm around her. We held each other so tightly I could feel her chest heaving, hear her quiet moans. I knew she was thinking about the loved ones she lost and the life she had lived. I yearned to soothe her sadness, to bring her back from the dark, from her recurrent nightmares.

Suddenly, she removed my arm from her shoulder and stepped back.

"It's okay," she said, wiping her tears with her faded blue and white chevron apron she always wore. "It's going to be fine. I am going to finish the dishes; tomorrow is another good day. We're going to sleep and it's going to be good."

I stood motionless, trying to make sense of my feelings. I had a sense that my mother did not want to dwell on her sadness or feel vulnerable – especially in front of me. And then, it came to me in a flash, I realized that my mother wanted me to be strong so I could protect myself in the face of adversity.

"I love you," was all I could muster.

CHAPTER TWENTY-TWO

The Trip to the Bank

When my father was stricken with Alzheimer's, my mom took over the family's finances. A bank manager came to our house to set up a bookkeeping system so she could keep track of checks, bank statements and other paperwork.

My mother slowly entered the numbers into the books with her impeccable handwriting, tallying up the figures and double checking the sums – and in her 80s, quickly became a competent bookkeeper.

Her financial skills often shocked many bankers who assumed she would be like other fragile, elderly women – too confused to handle their money. I had an opportunity to witness her financial skills in the spring of 2012, during *Purim*, when we drove up to Montreal for a visit.

My mom asked me to drive her to the bank, four blocks away from her house.

The bank hummed with activity. The line at the counter extended beyond the velvet dividing rope, as people awaited their turn, signed checks, filled out deposit slips, looked at their phones or just stared ahead. Tellers flipped through wads of bills, counting so rapidly that their thumbs looked blurred. The ATM machine whirred in the background with the promise of money to come.

"Oy," my mother sighed, glancing around the room for empty chairs.

Suddenly, a young man with a nametag appeared in front of us, presumably a financial advisor.

"Can I help you?" he said, looking sharp in his tailored suit, light blue shirt and lace-up shoes. "You don't have to wait in line."

He guided my mother by her elbow into his modular office, acknowledging me with a nod, and pointed to two chairs in front of a mahogany desk. He walked around the desk – its surface empty except for a card holder and a bowl of hard candy – and took his seat.

"What can I do for you?" he asked, sinking into the high-backed leather chair.

My mother explained she wanted to withdraw cash from her bank account and needed access to her safety deposit box.

Before giving him a chance to respond, she abruptly changed the subject.

"Tell me," she said slowly in her heavy Polish/Yiddish accent, staring at him, unblinkingly. "What *procentage* (that was how she pronounced percentage) can you give me for my money these days?"

The bank associate, startled by the non-sequitur, scratched his head, looking puzzled.

My mother pressed on. "I had my money in this bank but took most of it out because the other bank gave me more *procentage* points."

The adviser smiled, pleasantly surprised at her financial inquiry. "Let me call my manager," he said.

A few minutes later, the bank associate waltzed in with another dashing young man. The manager shook our hands, and my mother cut to the chase explaining she wanted to do business with the bank if the price was right.

The manager listened intently and then launched into his sales pitch, rattling off the different banking options such as higher interest accounts, instant credit approval.

He recommended my mom choose one of three investment

options, including a tax-deferred plan under which she would pay income tax at withdrawal rather than up-front.

"Tax deferred!" my mother jested. "Look at me, I'm already deferred!"

The two men seemed amused and impressed by my mother. They glanced at one another, then at my mom, and then at each other again.

The manager offered a rate.

"My mom waved away the offer. "Let's continue my business," she replied.

The manager shook her hand and walked away.

The associate turned to his computer explaining he was going to access her safety deposit box number.

"You need to look up my number?" my mother chuckled." I will tell you my number."

The associate led us into the vault locker. "Let me show you to your safety deposit box," he said.

"You have to show me where it is?" she added in good humor, clearly enjoying the conversation. "Come, and I will show you exactly where it is."

The associate smiled and, with a grand gesture, stepped aside to let her pass.

The last transaction transpired with no incident.

I put my arm around my mother, and we left the bank in high spirits. I felt so proud of my mother. Here was an 89-year-old woman, confident but unassuming, dazzling the two young bankers with her intelligence, business savvy and good humor!

I think back about our trip to the bank and smile, warmed by the memory.

CHAPTER TWENTY-THREE

The Phone Call

My mother and I phoned each other regularly for years. We talked about everything – what I was serving our guests for *Shabbos*, how I should renovate my kitchen, who was marrying whom. Often, I sought her advice and she told me what to do.

She was smart, perceptive and, although I did not always admit it, almost always right!

On a quiet Sunday afternoon in the Fall of 2012, after my husband and son left the house to play baseball in the park, I dialed her number for our routine chat.

"Ma," I greeted her enthusiastically, while wiping down the kitchen counter. "How are you?"

She did not respond right away.

"Who told you?" she shot back defensively, as if I had discovered a dark secret.

"Nobody told me anything," I said, gripping the phone, sensing that something was wrong. "I was just calling to say hello. Why, what happened?"

Again, silence. Thoughts about what could have happened to my mother flashed through my mind and my stomach tightened.

"I fell," she reported, flatly. "But I'm okay now."

I waited to hear more, but my mother did not elaborate.

"You fell, how?" I said, my voice frantic. "Why didn't you push the button to call for help?" I was referring to the medical alarm wristband my brothers and I insisted she wear since she was home alone. My father had already moved into a geriatric hospital near her home.

"Oy," she grumbled, "what do I need to push the button for? They are going to take me to the hospital and *damitche* (bother) me, pinching me with needles, *schlepping* (dragging) me to different rooms to test me for this and for that."

With some prompting she eventually described what happened.

She was apparently standing by the sink in the bathroom and then, suddenly, fell backward across the width of the bathtub, hitting her head on the faucet. She somehow landed crooked in the bathtub, arms and legs twisted.

"I gave myself a big *clop* (bang) in the head," she said.

My mom explained how she remained calm and tried out different positions to untangle herself and ease the pain.

"I saw that I could take care of myself," she continued. "I turned myself around to sit properly in the bathtub and sat for a good hour. I rested *mayne bayner* (my bones), then I saw I was okay to get up. I turned myself over onto my *k-nees* (knees), I held on to the tub ledge, got one foot up and then with the other I pushed myself up."

When she climbed out of the tub, she hobbled to the kitchen and called my sister-in-law, Ruchie, a physician who lived nearby. My mother assumed Ruchie told me what happened – but that was not the case.

I did not appreciate the severity of the fall until I visited her in Montreal a few weeks later: She had a huge bump on her head and blackened bruises covering the left side of her body from the chest down.

When my mother was in pain she rarely complained. When she was diagnosed with pancreatic cancer, for instance, her aides were the last to know until the disease was so advanced that she had to be hospitalized. My brother, a physician, said most people would have gone into the hospital months earlier.

My mother never expected us, however, to keep our pain to ourselves. When we fell and cried as kids, my mother treated us with kid gloves. I remember bursting through our front door with scarred knees, bloody scrapes. "We'll fix it," she reassured me in a calm, smooth voice, gently guiding me to the bathroom where the medical supplies were kept. My sobs subsided into whimpers as she cleaned my wounds with hydrogen peroxide, dabbed them with antibiotic ointment to prevent infection and applied Band-Aids over the injury.

"You will be okay," she continued. "And I will take care of it."

And she did take care of us then and for the rest of her life.

I grew up thinking my mother could move mountains. Many decades later, I questioned her physical strength to move around but never her willpower. Her presence always loomed large in my life and still does today, eight years after her passing.

CHAPTER TWENTY-FOUR

A Magical Seder

My mom placed one hand on her heart, the other over my shoulder.

"Oy," she said on our way home from my friend Helena's house, where we celebrated the first night of Passover. The streets were cold, and my mother was bundled up.

"This is an unbelievable night. Can you believe that the boy – your friend Ilana's son – came to me and asked *me* for a *bracha* (blessing) to get married to the right person?"

She stopped. Took a deep breath. Looked up at the sky.

"Can you imagine," she beamed, "people used to call my *bubbe* Ziesl to ask her for blessings. Now, after so many years, a boy who doesn't even know me asks *me* for a *bracha*!"

The boy she was referring to was Bradley, a yeshiva student and my friend's son. Bradley wanted my mother's blessing because he was impressed by the knowledge, wisdom, and compassion my mother displayed while discussing the *Haggadah*, the Jewish text that commemorates the Israelites' exodus from Egypt.

My friend, Helena, invited about 20 people to the *Seder*, a mix of neighborhood friends and family. My mom, who visited us from Montreal for *Pesach*, came along. *Pesach* was the holiday that resonated with her the most since she believed that God protected her from the Nazis just as He protected the Israelites from the Egyptians.

We arrived at Helena's house, a large, three-story brick colonial in a quiet tree-lined street, as men were returning from services. She directed us to the dining room table, elegantly set with fine china and artfully decorated *Seder* plates.

Helena's husband, Jay, who led the *Seder*, poured the first cup of wine and recited the *Kiddush*, the blessing over the wine, continuing the Jewish tradition that began more than 3,500 years ago. Other blessings followed.

Next came the retelling of the Passover story. We went around the table taking turns reading the *Haggadah*, stopping frequently to ask questions or make comments on the text. Everyone had a lot to say as we all explored rich themes such as redemption, freedom, and miracles.

My mother, educated in Jewish texts, jumped right in.

She spoke with passion, conviction, and determination, citing Biblical sources and other references.

The men listened to her, nodding slowly in agreement, glancing at each other and marveling at the scholarship of the 89-year-old woman. Mesmerized by my mother's comments, Bradley sat still, leaning forward, absorbing every word.

When the *Seder* was over, he approached her. I inched my way toward them to listen to their conversation and heard my mother recite a prayer.

"The *Ribbono Shel Olam* (Master of the Universe) should give you health, happiness and all the things you ask for. He should send you the right *zivug* (match) and you should live happily together and raise beautiful children. I wish you *bracha* (blessing), *hatzlacha* (success), *gezunt* (health) and *parnassah* (sustenance)."

My eyes swelled with tears. My mother was proud of her *yichus*, her pedigree, the prominent position her family held in the community in Poland before the war. As a Holocaust survivor who lost her entire family except her father, she felt responsible for carrying on the family name. But when she moved to Canada with my *zeide*, penniless and alone, her distinguished ancestry was known to no one.

And then Bradley came along. He admired her knowledge and devotion, her commitment to performing *mitzvos*, and her strong sense of purpose. He saw something in her, a glimmer of her great past.

Bradley's request for a blessing turned an already wonderful evening into a magical night.

CHAPTER TWENTY-FIVE

Liya

*K*atya and Matewka Budniewski saved my mother's life — but their daughter Liya captured my mother's heart.

Liya was a miracle child — the child my mother prayed the Budniewskis would conceive after years of infertility. Prayers were all my mother could offer, she told the Budniewskis before going into hiding, in exchange for their generosity.

When Matewka wrote a note to my mother announcing Katya's pregnancy, my mother heaved a sigh of relief. She knew the Budniewskis would continue hiding her because they believed in the power of her prayer despite the lethal penalties the Nazis imposed on those who harbored Jews.

Liya, 1964.

With life growing in Katya's womb, the Budniewskis risked their own lives to protect my mother.

My mother corresponded with Liya for over 60 years, reveling in Liya's successes, mourning over her sorrows. Every small achievement loomed large in my mother's eyes. She marveled at Liya's penmanship.

"Oy, I heard from Liya today," she once exclaimed, shaking a letter in front of me. "Look at her beautiful handwriting." I gazed at the neatly written words in Russian, the language my mother taught herself while in hiding.

My mother knew that Liya struggled to make ends meet in an economically depressed Ukraine, often ravaged by war and scarcity. To alleviate her burdens, my mother often sent Liya money and clothing packages.

"This is for Liya and her family," I recall her saying one afternoon, placing neatly folded gently worn sweaters into a box — her packing precise, efficient, not an inch to spare.

On her death, my mother worried about Liya's future. She asked me to reach out to her and help her whenever necessary.

The opportunity to take over my mother's labor of love presented itself immediately.

While my mother was in the hospital, shortly before her death, I received a Skype message from Tamara, a friend of Liya who spoke English and agreed to serve as Liya's translator. Liya, Tamara said, had been trying to reach my mother to tell her she suffered injuries in a car crash and needed an operation — but nobody answered the phone. By the time I had the chance to call Liya to explain the situation, my mother had passed away.

My Russian hairdresser agreed to serve as a translator in the 3-way call.

"Liya," I exclaimed, "this is Sandy, Freda's daughter." Flushed with emotion, I extolled the virtues of her parents who saved my mother at all costs, words of love spilling from my lips. I then choked up. My voice cracked as I delivered the heartbreaking news.

Silence on the other end. Then Liya, clearing her voice, expressed condolences, and tenderly shared how much her parents loved my mother.

I listened, my heart softening at the sound of her sweet faraway voice, trying to grasp the enormity of this encounter. I kept thinking to myself: *This is Liya in the flesh and blood! The Liya my mother loved, the Liya born from my mother's prayer, the Liya delivered by God to save her.* How I yearned to travel through the sound waves and touch the face of the woman whose birth reassured my mother's life.

I then asked Liya what I could do to help her with her medical care — making good on the promise I made to my mother.

Over the next few months, we exchanged Skype messages often, with Tamara as our intermediary. I learned that Liya was a pathologist who worked in a morgue, a red brick building next to the infectious disease wing of a hospital. She loved books about art and history and owned an impressive library. She relished entertaining, delighting her guests with delicacies she baked from her aunt's recipes.

I explained to Liya that my mother dictated her memoir to me in the last three months of her life, detailing her experiences during the war and praising the heroic acts of Liya's parents who risked everything to save her. I asked for details about her parents' life so I could include it in the book and told her she would get a copy once published.

Liya subsequently underwent surgery. I envisioned flying Liya to the US after she recovered, lavishing her with love and affection and feeling my mother's presence in the giving.

But my euphoria vanished, my heart plunged.

I received a Skype message from Tamara reporting that Liya was diagnosed with cancer and died suddenly.

My heart dropped and I felt adrift. Liya was the last living person linked to my mother's survival during the war — and that link was now severed.

Tamara's words were consoling. "Liya left us after learning about the death of your mother. And just as Liya came into this world with the arrival of your mother into her family, Liya left this world along with your mother."

I looked at the date of her death and froze: She died on December 13, 2014, within the week that my brothers stopped saying the *Mourner's Kaddish* for my mother, a prayer recited for 11 months, during which, according to Jewish custom, the soul completes its ascent to heaven.

I imagined Liya stepping into heaven, sliding into my mother's warm embrace.

While clearing out my mother's house, I came across photos of Liya slipped in between pieces of cardboard my mother recycled from packages to prevent wrinkling. In one black and white picture, Liya, maybe six or so, looked slightly away from the camera, her braided hair parted on the side, tucked neatly behind her ear. Then a slightly older Liya, maybe in her teens, with a beehive hair style typical of the time, her lips parted in a gentle smile.

Liya, my mother's angel. I imagine my mother's love radiating around Liya in the vast expanse of a heavenly world we will all one day inhabit, their relationship born in war now blessed with peace, their future in God's hands.

In this image, I find comfort.

CHAPTER TWENTY-SIX

Dad

*A*s I was nearing the completion of this book, I realized that a book about my mom could not be complete without describing her life's partner of 62 years - my dad. They were so intimately connected that my father was always there with her in the nightmares that she suffered since the war, despite them having met and married afterwards. Indeed, one cannot remember my mother without the acknowledgement of her dear Mendel. I therefore now include some detail as to who this wonderful man was as a person, a husband, a father, a businessman, a community man, and as a family man.

Mendel Schipper, Stuttgart, 1947.

My father was born on March 25, 1921 to Chaim and Sarah Schipper in Wolica, a small village in Przeworsk County in Galicia, Poland. There were few Jews in Wolica, so my father and his brother, Hersh (Herman), had many Christian friends. Dad and his family's happy and uneventful *shtetl* life ended abruptly – as it did for so many others – with the Nazi invasion of Poland in 1939. Unlike my mother, my father was reticent to recount his wartime experiences, preferring to shield his children from the evils that befell him and his family during the war.

I regret not having learned much about my father's survival. Thankfully, he briefly shared a few stories, permitting a glimpse into the horrors and his subsequent bravery at that time.

Separated from other family members, my father, and his brother, Hersh, were sent to the Pustkow labor camp. Remarkably, it was a young German officer, the son of a high-ranking German official, who helped the two brothers while they were in the labor camp. In his search of a German speaking prisoner who could act as his translator, the German officer found my father. My father was hauled up onto the officer's horse and they rode around together, with my father offering his assistance where needed. The officer took a liking to the blue-eyed, blond-haired, Jewish boy and in an unprecedented act of humanity, armed my father with a pistol. Later, the brothers made their daring escape from the camp's infirmary.

For the duration of the war, my father and his brother hid in the woods among the Polish resistance fighters, many of whom had been their friends before the war. This would explain the acceptance of the Jewish brothers by the often-antisemitic Partisans.

Armed with the gun they received from the officer, Hersh and Dad procured food by robbing the fields of the Polish peasants. Without this sustenance, the two brothers would have surely starved to death.

During the war, my father boldly attended the wedding of a friend's sister, staying only a short time and dancing with the bride. Although the other guests knew him as the Jewish thug who was robbing the farmers, the sheer audacity of Dad's appearance further showcased his bravado. On another occasion, my father courageously left the woods for the nearby town of Urzejowice to bring some food to his cousins, the Engelbergs. Although he did not find them at that time because they had gone into hiding, he did manage to help them at the war's conclusion, when Poles were murdering Jews due to antisemitism and out of concern that the Jews would reclaim their property.

My cousin, Sally Engelberg Frishberg, whose father was a first cousin to my father, recounted to me the frightening day the Polish marauders came to her house, fired a warning shot that whizzed by her mother's ear, and threatened to return and kill them if they did not leave town. This prompted Sally and her family to leave immediately, making their way from one town to the next before finding safety in a DP camp. It was years later, when talking to my father, that she learned why she had received the "generous" warning to vacate her home. When my father heard that his "friends," the Polish partisans, were planning to murder the Jews in their town, he beseeched them to spare the lives of Sally and her family, pleading that they instead chase his relatives from their town. As Sally recently told me, "There is no doubt in my mind that your father's actions saved my life and the lives of my family."

After the war, my father spent several years in Munich, Germany and immigrated to Canada in 1950, with the help of Karol Mozdzen, his Polish Catholic friend living in Sault-St-Marie, Ontario. Following several years in Winnipeg and Toronto, at the age of 30, he moved to Montreal to marry my mother. Their dreams of creating a family came true and from the years 1954 to 1960, they became the parents they dreamed of becoming.

**

My father came to the shores of North America virtually penniless. Nevertheless, his drive to support his family and provide for the education of his three children, his formidable work ethic, and a healthy dose of *Hakaras HaTov* (gratitude) for his "second life" in Canada, allowed him to escape poverty and prosper. These accomplishments brought him considerable pride and satisfaction. The process, however, was gradual and painstaking – first as a mechanic assembling engine parts at Canadair, then as a shareholder in the

Canadian Outfitting department store, and finally as a successful builder in the construction business with his life-long and cherished business partners, Abram Neuman, Yakob Yakubovitch and Joe Bultz. Although denied a formal education, the partners would rely on Mendel Schipper to detect potential weaknesses in business contracts overlooked by lawyers. My father nurtured excellent relationships with co-workers and clients of every denomination. He was scrupulously honest, and everyone knew it. His spoken word and a handshake at the Bank of Montreal carried the weight of signed documents.

Mendel was a man with integrity which formed the fulcrum of everything he did. The decency, goodness, and honesty he exhibited to his family and others were exemplary, and his moral character was often remarked upon by friends, acquaintances, and business affiliates.

A handsome man with sapphire blue eyes and a smile as big as the sky and as warm as the sun, my father embodied the teachings in *Pirkei Avos* 1:15[1] which states *"Emor me'at v'oseh harbei"* (Say little and do a lot). He let his actions speak louder than his words.

His compassion, grace, and respect for others was epitomized in the way he treated and respected my mother's father, Nosson Nuta Perelmuter, who lived in our home. It was out of respect that my father gave up his seat at the head of our table to my grandfather, and it was my grandfather who led us in all the holiday ceremonies and customs. Although my father was raised in an Orthodox home, he extended himself beyond his personal comfort zone to accommodate my *zeide*'s high standard of religious observance. Such was the respect my father had for my grandfather that in all my years living at home, I never heard my father raise his voice to my *zeide*.

When my grandfather was diagnosed with esophageal cancer, it was my father who took him to all his treatments, ensuring that he was getting the best care possible. And when my *zeide* passed

---

[1] *Pirkei Avos* (Ethics of our Fathers) is a tractate of the *Mishna*, which is the codification of the Jewish oral laws.

away in 1979 at age 82, my father cried uncontrollably. It was the first time *ever* I saw my father cry.

Prior to his passing, my *zeide* had arranged for his dear friend, Rabbi Leib Kramer[2] *z"l*, to say the Mourner's Kaddish (a prayer to honor the deceased, recited for eleven months during the three daily prayer services) and in exchange for this deed, he bequeathed all of his *seforim* (sacred texts) to the Rabbi. After my *zeide*'s passing, my father insisted on saying Kaddish for his father-in-law. When Rabbi Kramer observed how heartfelt and diligent Dad was in performing this mitzvah, he returned all my *zeide*'s *seforim* to our family. The collection is now proudly displayed in my brother Chaim's home.

My grandfather's presence was an enormous blessing to our family for which my father deserved much credit.

***

With custom-tailored suits hung meticulously in the closet and ties lined up on the tie rack or returned to the plastic sleeves in which they were originally purchased, my father gleaned much enjoyment from the things he could finally afford. Similarly, he wanted to give his children everything he did not have which included material things, education, and the ability to live life to the fullest.

In our home, the Canadian Outfitting Department Store where my dad worked came to be known as "*dem* store" (the store), regardless of whether my parents were speaking English or Yiddish - like "*Vus a tsayt kumst tu ahaym fun dem* store?" (What time are you coming home from the store?)

Thursday nights were late nights at *dem* store where my dad met with clients looking to buy merchandise. So, when I was permitted, I would excitedly join my dad with the expectation of doing some shopping. The two hours of carsickness I had to endure while my

---

[2] Rabbi Leib Kramer, a native of Chelm, Poland like my grandfather, was the founder of the first Lubavitch yeshiva in Canada. He was a longtime director of the Chabad institutions in Montreal, and a legendary figure in the Montreal Jewish community.

dad drove house-to-house collecting money from his clients prior to arriving at the department store, could not dampen my anticipation of this shopping expedition. I have vivid memories of watching him from the car as he sprinted up the outdoor, spiral, metal staircases (unique to vintage Montreal) often skipping over one or two steps, leading to their apartments.

Once arriving at the multi-level building on St Lawrence Blvd, my father busied himself with customers. I used that opportunity to make my way to the second floor where I entertained myself touring the numerous aisles of children's clothing, trying on and selecting the items I liked best and making my own purchases.

When I was done shopping, I, together with my over-sized, string-tied, brown paper-wrapped package, would find my father, and patiently wait for him to finish his business before returning home. Can you imagine how much fun this was for a young girl?

At home, my mother would often insist that some of the items I purchased be repackaged and returned the following day. But when I modeled my new purchases for my father, the familiar smile of delight would wash over his face. Shimmering so brightly, I could see my reflection in his big blue eyes. This expression of satisfaction and pride in seeing me in my new outfits let me know, without a doubt, that I would get to keep *all* my purchases!

***

Although children of Holocaust survivors share many similarities, I have learned that vast and unique differences exist, depending on how acclimated to their new lives the parents became after the war. Growing up on a street with other Holocaust survivors we forged one huge family, and we, the children, were tasked with the responsibility of nudging our parents towards socially accepted behaviors and norms. Since they looked to each other for parenting skills, we only had to convince one set of parents and the others would follow suit.

All the parents on our street wanted their children to live the lives they never had, and so we were never given the social restrictions common to other children of Holocaust survivors. This is not to say that my parents did not imbue me with the usual fears and trepidations common to survivors, but despite those warnings, I could live my life. For example, I never had a curfew. Since Montreal events and parties started late at night, it was okay for me to return home in the early morning hours if I was with my friends. It was comforting to be so trusted by my parents.

One night, while attending a party at McGill University, I embarrassingly tore my pants. I was having so much fun that night and my friends and I were not ready to leave the party. But I desperately needed a change of clothes! Although it was around 2:00 am, I did not hesitate to call, wake my parents, and explain the situation. Immediately, my dad agreed to bring me another pair of pants, so he dressed and drove the twenty-minute ride to the university. You would think he would have insisted that I come home, but you would be wrong. When he arrived, he handed me another pair of pants and waited for me to change. He then gave me a big hug and told me to be careful and enjoy myself. This illustrated how much he wanted me to have fun and be happy, and how much he trusted me.

* * *

My father was a homebody, valuing the comforts of our home over going out. This did not mean he was antisocial, as he had many friends and was highly active in our synagogue, serving as a member of the Board of Governors. Because he was always the first to arrive, my father was given the keys to the *shul* and tasked with unlocking the doors for the daily, early morning prayers.

Together, my parents had a mutual devotion to our shul and the community. While my father shared in the responsibility of the strategic functions of the synagogue and was a daily participant for prayers, my mother was active in the women's group, discussing the weekly *parsha* (*Torah* portion) and related subjects. At home, while he worked on business related matters, she could often be seen sitting in her favorite living room chair, preparing her notes for the upcoming women's group meeting. She was often referred to as *the Rebbetzin*, not because she was the wife of a rabbi, but rather as an honorific title acknowledging her elevated status in the learning group.

Besides his involvement with our synagogue, there were a few other things that my father enjoyed outside of the home – our Sunday day trips in the summers to the beaches in Plattsburgh and Messina when we were young, our weekly Sunday night dinner outings, and Western movies. Unlike my mother, who could not stand to witness any more fighting, shootings and killings, my father loved Western movies, so he would *shlep* my mother to see them. Occasionally, I would watch my parents dress in their finest attire to attend a wedding or Bar Mitzvah party, a New Year's Eve party, an Israel Bond Drive dinner, or other fundraisers they deemed important. But most of the time, my parents were at home, happy to have meals with their children and perhaps watch a little television.

In the '60s and '70s , Sunday nights at 9:00pm were reserved for watching one of my father's favorite television shows, *Bonanza*. Dad enjoyed watching the ethical Ben Cartwright (played by Lorne Greene) as the patriarch of a Nevada ranching family, in which he and his sons, Adam, Hoss and Little Joe (Pernell Roberts, Dan Blocker, and Michael Landon) were always victorious against the deviant elements of society. Set in the 1860s, the show was known for presenting moral dilemmas in which the good guys were always triumphant over the bad guys. My dad identified with this morality story where honest and noble virtues were depicted as important.

Besides *Bonanza*, his other favorite television shows were the five seasons of the WWII drama series, *Combat!*, which ran from 1962 to 1967, the 1967 movie entitled *The Dirty Dozen*, and the series which followed in 1988 by the same name. Nothing pleased my father more than watching the 'dispatching' of dozens of high-ranking Nazi officers.

As time passed and life improved for my parents, we began to take family vacations. The first was a road trip to New York City, followed by a trip to Atlantic City the following year. Subsequently, we spent two weeks every summer at the all-inclusive resorts in the Catskill Mountains, with Grossinger's being my parents' favorite. In the *Borscht Belt*, as it was known, they enjoyed the country air, the delicious and plentiful food, and the comedy acts including, Milton Berle, Jackie Mason, Jerry Lewis, and Sid Caeser. Later, they would spend a couple of weeks during the winter at their favorite Miami Beach haunt – The Caribbean Hotel. There, they looked forward to meeting up with friends, many of them Holocaust survivors, from Montreal and the U.S. eastern seaboard.

Devoted to the nascent State of Israel and the Jewish people, my parents made numerous trips to Israel, both privately and as a part of organized missions with the Beth Zion Synagogue and with the Emunah organization. They both enjoyed meeting the average Israeli on the street as well as the prominent political and rabbinic personalities.

Growing up in our home, the *mitzvah* of *Hachnasat Orchim* (deed of showing hospitality) was an integral part of our lives. This was attributed to the open house and welcoming atmosphere my parents maintained. Guests were regularly invited, and we often had visitors for *Shabbos* (the Sabbath) and holidays. In the summer of 1967, our basement was strewn with wall-to-wall mattresses and bedding to accommodate all the guests we hosted for the Expo '67 fair.

***

To provide his family with a comfortable life, Dad worked hard to earn his money, always striving to do better, but never compromising who he was as a person. When he worked the graveyard shift at the civil and military aircraft company, Canadair, the union shop steward told him to slow down because he was producing four times that of the day shift workers! Dad was furious because he felt that the steward should have instructed the day shift workers to work faster. It was from this experience that my father developed his dislike of unions.

Prosperity further improved for my parents when my father secured a $500 loan and partnered with another Holocaust survivor, Phillip Fulton, to buy a full share in the Canadian Outfitting Company. As mentioned earlier in this book, the shareholders were responsible for selling products on credit to clients in the store, and for the weekly collection of payments from these clients at their homes. My father worked at the Canadian Outfitting for many years. Although he often came home late at night, my mother was always there to greet him with a warm, home-cooked meal.

In 1968, with some savings, my father purchased a parcel of land with three other Holocaust survivors and proceeded to build and sell a house. With the profits from this transaction, the partners purchased more property, thus launching the Adiro Construction Company that the partners operated for decades. The company is named for the beautiful Adirondack Mountains located in upstate New York.

Most of the properties the company built were in the Italian neighborhoods of St. Leonard and Montreal North. The partners earned the reputation for quality construction, honesty, and integrity. Once, when trying to negotiate with a new drywall supplier, the supplier insisted on upfront payment. Upon hearing that no credit was offered to Adiro by the supplier, Adiro's largest competitor in the area told the supplier that he would "personally guarantee Schipper's credit."

A young, Italian couple once came to see one of Adiro's newly constructed houses. They obviously liked the house but were not comfortable with the price. My father was unwilling to lower the price any further, and so they left. The couple, however, returned the following week, with the bride's father in tow. Once again, the young man tried to negotiate the price, but Dad held firm. All the while, the father-in-law remained silent. Finally, the young man said that he would only entertain the asking price if the developer would install ample insulation. "I do not want my kids to get cold when they're playing on the floor of the basement," he told Dad. My father had the man follow him to the basement, where he instructed him to lift some of the floorboards to see that the requested insulation was already installed. Seeing the insulation already there, the young man exclaimed incredulously, "You installed the insulation as part of the base build?", to which my dad replied, "I don't want your kids to be cold either." Finally, the old father spoke up. He said, "Giuseppe.... sign!"

The partners moved from building duplexes and triplexes to condo towers and apartment buildings. They named one of their condo towers *Quadomaine* because they liked the beach project in Hollywood, Florida which bore the name. They were unaware that the name means *four domains* which was not well-suited for their single tower building. Nevertheless, Adiro's Quadomaine project was quite successful.

Mendel was a self-taught man, having never completed schooling beyond the seventh grade. Upon arriving in Canada, he had to learn both English and French, and because he worked predominantly in Italian neighborhoods, Dad picked up conversational Italian as well. He taught himself how to read blueprints and became adept at sifting through legal documents. In one transaction, my father appeared at the bank together with his lawyer to negotiate the terms of a mortgage with the bank manager and the bank's attorney. After reviewing the documents, Dad's lawyer confirmed that they were in order, but before he could slide them over to the bank's attorney, my father intercepted the documents and proceeded to make several important revisions. The bank accepted all the revisions, and as the meeting concluded, the bank's lawyer leaned over to my father and whispered "Mr. Schipper ... well done!"

Over time, Dad and his partners got out of the residential real estate business and together with another Holocaust survivor, Ralph Cynader, began purchasing commercial real estate. These properties were mainly located in the Greater Montreal area, but also in the United States. In one such transaction, the availability of the partners' Canadian funds was delayed for a day or so beyond the closing date. Astonishingly, upon the reputation of Mendel Schipper, the bank manager proceeded to forward the funds to the US bank, trusting that he would receive the Canadian capital promptly. The transaction was conducted without a hitch, and the bank's trust was not disappointed.

I was so proud of my father for having mastered the skills needed to build a successful business. Mostly, I admired his kindness, integrity, generosity, and quiet intellect. You can imagine how sad it was when years later my father developed Alzheimer's, which robbed him of his capacity to think, communicate, and care for himself. When my mother could no longer care for him at home, he moved to Maimonides Geriatric Hospital in Cote St. Luc, a few blocks away from our house. It was gut-wrenching for all of us to witness his inability to recognize the family he spent his whole life nurturing. Seeing how kindly he treated the nurses and how appreciative he was of their care, gave me glimpses of the noble personality that still sparkled within the shell.

My father spent four years in Maimonides and my mother visited daily, bringing him his favorite home-made cakes and pastries. When his appetite diminished, it was my mother who sat patiently beside him together with his aide, trying her best to feed him and keep him well nourished. It was only in her final weeks that my mother was unable to visit. I am certain that he felt her absence. He died just three months after her passing.

When I was sitting *shiva* for my dad, a friend by the name of Marty Lieberman came to visit. My father had business dealings with Marty's father, Aharon. Marty told me a story I had never heard before.

Our two fathers had a deal together - my father was selling a building to his father. They had agreed on the price with a handshake. A short time later, though, my father was offered considerably more for the building. Having made the verbal agreement with

Aharon, Mendel refused to entertain the better offer and did not try to renegotiate the deal. This made such an impression on Aharon that he shared this story of my father's integrity with his son, Marty. Hearing this story from Marty was uplifting and inspirational. It was the quintessential portrait of the ethics of my loving father.

My mother and father survived the persecution and attempted annihilation by the Nazis to build a loving home together in Canada and become exemplary role models to their children. They taught us the paramount values of a life lived with integrity and grace, a loving, committed marriage, love of God and Israel, and perpetual respect for others.

With them gone, the world is not the same.

I miss them terribly and I carry them in my heart, always.

In Memoriam

On January 27, 2014 (26th of Shevat, 5774), my mother, Fradl Perelmuter Schipper, *z"l*, passed away. She was my hero, my champion, and the beating heart of our family.

"My Yiddishe momme, there's nothing better in this world…"

Her *yahrzeit* (anniversary of her death) shares the same date as that of the Radziner Rebbe, Rabbi Mordechai Yosef Elazar Leiner, *ztz"l*, the *"Tiferes Yosef"* (26th of Shevat, 5689).

Three months later, my mother was reunited with her life's partner when my father, Menachem Mendel Schipper, *z"l*, passed away on May 1, 2014 (2nd of Iyar, 5774).

My parents are buried in the Baron De Hirsch Cemetery in Montreal. It was my mother's wish to memorialize her family members who perished in the Holocaust, by inscribing their names on the back of her *matzevah* (gravestone). Although they were never afforded proper burials, at least a gravestone now marks their names.

GOLDBER
FREDA PERELMUTTER SCHIPPER
MENDEL SCHIPPER
שיפער
שיפער
FREDA PERELMUTTER
SCHIPPER
JAN. 3. 1923–JAN. 27. 2014
BELOVED WIFE, MOTHER
AND GRANDMOTHER
MENDEL
SCHIPPER
MAR. 25. 1921–MAY 1. 2014
BELOVED HUSBAND, FATHER
AND GRANDFATHER

Legacy

"The legacy of heroes is the memory of a great name and the inheritance of a great example."

–Benjamin Disraeli
1804-1881

This book is a timely testimony of the accounts of my mother during the darkest days of human history. It is important to make these events known considering today's rising antisemitism. Freda devoted much of her life recollecting the Holocaust and teaching its lessons to all who would listen, precisely because she anticipated the virulent Holocaust denial and revisionism that dares to repudiate these truths.

Although her lineage was nearly severed, my mother spared no effort in relaying her story to us, her treasured legacy. Both of my parents would have taken much delight in seeing our families now, and they forever remain an integral part in all our lives.

Chaim Schipper and Family.
Left to right: Tani, Ruchie, Chaim, and Dovid. Montreal, 2021.

Sandy Schipper Wolberg and Family.
Left to right: Sandy, George and Jeffrey. New York, 2021.

Saul Schipper and Family.
Left to right: Zoe, Mayah, Stephanie, Saul, Danielle, and Sarah. Montreal, 2021.

Appendices

APPENDIX I

Freda's Poetry

The following is a collection of poems originally written in Polish and Yiddish by my mother while she hid in the pit under the Budniewskis' barn. The first poem was translated in Montreal by her friend, Leah Kaufman. Trying to stay as true to her original poems as possible, I translated the next three poems from the Yiddish version that my mother submitted to the Horodlo *Yizkor* book, *Kehilat Horodlo*.

Attached to one of these three poems entitled "I Long for Home," I found a note from my mother explaining that she wrote this poem in the voice of her eldest brother, Moshe Levi Yitzchak. In the hope of finding safety, he had crossed the Bug River to stay with family living in Volodymyr, Ukraine. He was shot and buried alive in a mass grave together with 200 other Jewish boys near the Volodymyr prison on *Erev Yom Kippur*, September 30, 1941, at age twenty.

A Prayer from Within the Cave

O rise up my God-fearing mother,
And observe reality now,
How our Jewish blood fills the seas,
Please, beg God to save your last surviving child somehow.

The world is so filled with beauty,
That is not mine to behold,
I hide in this cave hidden
And shiver, so lonely, so frightened, and so cold.

I need you near, my dearest mother,
To run, intervene to the God above,
That my anguish should not be in vain,
Please, plead for me mamma, for compassion and love.

Please rise my young, martyred brothers,
And be silent no more,
Yell to the Heavens above you,
Your innocent blood should not be spilled in vain on the floor.

Arm yourselves with weapons dear brothers,
And declare on the enemy war,
Destroy the land of the Germans!
May they never find the peace they had before this war.

I Long for Home

The Germans came into our town
and slaughtered us with rage.
On the Russian side I hunkered down
and separated from my mommenu at such a young age.

Like some joke it felt when I had to leave
my sweet and beautiful home.
So many years it was hard to believe
I would not see my mommenu, I would be alone.

Letters filled with misery I received
of torture, humiliation, and persecution.
In the house with the children she lies aggrieved,
her life full of hardship and destitution.

The world was once a peaceful and better place,
my home, an enormous pleasure.
Like a dream it all passed at such a brisk pace.
These memories I will always treasure.

The shtetl I am from I must remember.
How beautiful my home – a gem!
My gut-wrenching longing for my mother, my mentor.
When will I see it all again?

The Bug River border where I stand alone
at the river's shore.
Let me go to Horodlo, my shtetl, my home.
Let this tyranny be no more.

The war created our terrible plight.
Upon us the sun did set.
I search for those old times filled with light
That we shall meet as once we met.

A Tearful Story

A very sad song I would like to sing.
My heart has turned to stone.
All over the world alarms should ring
about the murderers who would not leave us alone.

How the Germans came to our homes and towns,
no one could comprehend.
How they robbed us of our lives and surrounds,
and gratuitously slaughtered us in the streets until our bitter end.

Our murderers wanted our immediate identification.
White armbands we were ordered to wear.
Our faces burned with deep humiliation,
as our mothers and fathers walked on in despair.

So much of their time they spent in thought
of how to rid the Jews in short duration.
And to the ghettos we were brought,
and left to die of starvation.

To the work camps they grabbed and sent our men,
who were starved and tortured relentlessly.
They beat, abused, and tormented them
until a dark death became their destiny.

They attacked us and we were so shaken
as they chased us from our homes.
To the trains in Miaczyn we were taken
Woe! What happened there – no one would ever know!

They separated us from our fathers and mothers
and we stood witness to all the violence.
In front of our eyes they killed half the others.
We gritted our teeth as we stood in silence.

A dark gloomy train arrived at the station.
Oh, why did all this even start?
Forced onto the train without hesitation,
I saw my mother and my siblings soon depart.

Oh, woe is me! This life so saddened.
Alone like a stone I remain.
I could never have quite imagined
that I would never see my mother again.

Lonesome and desolate we now remain
No home, no fathers, no mothers.
All our strength had been utterly drained
and hard labor was forced upon me and the others.

From the sky a fiery star did fall,
tearing the earth asunder.
With one fell swoop chaos reigned overall,
obliterating our glory and wonder.

What will become of us when our work is finished?
The murderer has ordered us shot and killed.
His bandits obey with great zeal and relish,
and our young Jewish blood will forever be spilled.

Oh God! See our tears and feel our desperation,
our anguish and our pain.
Intercede on our behalf and for our future generations.
Will salvation come? When will we be free again?

I cried a pool of tears in which all could swim,
and God helped me in my time of need.
The gentile, Budniewski, took me in
and saved me from death, this man of word and deed.

APPENDIX II

Favorite Yiddish Idioms

*M*y mother was a wonderful communicator because of her intellect, wit and her keen ability to masterfully capture subtle nuances and respond appropriately. Speaking in sentences that often began in English and concluded in Yiddish, she used her vast cache of Yiddish idioms to express complex ideas, to amplify messages, and to add humor and color to her conversations.

The following idioms are just a sample of her most memorable ones, but nowhere near the countless collection she sprinkled into her everyday speech:

אויפן גנב ברענט דאס היטל
Oyfn ganev brent dos hitl
TRANSLATION: The hat burns on the thief
MEANING: A thief's guilty conscience will betray him

....

אז גאט וויל, שיסט א בעזעם
Az Got vil, shist a bezem
TRANSLATION: If God wants, a broom shoots
MEANING: Anything can happen if God wants it to

....

אבי מען לעבט
Abi men lebt
TRANSLATION & MEANING: At least we're alive

....

אז מען לעבט דערלעבט מען
Az men lebt derlebt men
TRANSLATION: When one lives, one lives to experience
MEANING: When one lives long enough, one lives to experience incredible things

....

א זוינס און א זעלעכס
A zoyns un a zelechs

TRANSLATION:
Such a thing and such a thing
MEANING:
Outstanding

אידישע הארץ
Yiddishe hartz
TRANSLATION:
Jewish heart
MEANING:
Merciful heart

איין מאל אין א יובל
Ayn mol in a yoyvel
TRANSLATION:
Once in a Jubilee year
MEANING:
Very infrequently

אן אלטער בער קען מען נישט לערנען טאנצן
An alter ber ken men nisht lernen tantsn
TRANSLATION:
You can't teach an old bear to dance
MEANING:
You can't teach an old dog new tricks

אונגעבלאזן ווי אן אינדיק
Ungeblozn vi an indik
TRANSLATION:
Puffed up like a turkey
MEANING:
Irritable and sulking personality

אונשיקעניש
Unshikenish
TRANSLATION AND MEANING:
An affliction, curse, or nuisance; an irksome, troublesome thing or person

ארעם ווי די נאכט
Orem vi di nacht
TRANSLATION:
Poor as night
MEANING:
Extremely poor

אראפ פון בוידעם
Arop fun boydem
TRANSLATION:
Fell out of the attic
MEANING:
(He/she is) nuts, nonsense

אוי געוואלד און געשריגן
Oy gevald aun geshrign
TRANSLATION:
An expression of outrage and yelling
MEANING:
Used to express shock or amazement

א נעכטיגן טאג
A nechtign tog
TRANSLATION:
A yesterday's day
MEANING:
It's untrue; it didn't happen; impossible

אויף אלע מיינע שונאים געזאגט
Oyf ale mayne sonim gezugt
TRANSLATION:
It should be said on all my enemies
MEANING:
I wish it on all my enemies

א נאר בלייבט א נאר
A nar blaybt a nar
TRANSLATION AND MEANING:
A fool remains a fool

א שטעקן האט צוויי עקן
A shtekn hot tsvey ekn
TRANSLATION:
A stick has two ends
MEANING:
It's a double-edged sword.

א כשר'ן טאפ מיט א כשר'ן לעפל
A kosheren top mit a kosheren lefl
TRANSLATION:
A kosher pot with a kosher spoon
MEANING:
It all worked out well; it's all legal

אלץ ביי איינעם איז נישט דא ביי קיינעם
Alts bay eynem is nisht du bay keynem
TRANSLATION:
Everything in one person doesn't exist in anybody
MEANING:
No one has it all

אויס כלה צוריק מויד
Oys kallah tsurik moyd
TRANSLATION:
No more bride, back to being a regular girl
MEANING:

Mom's Yiddish Idioms

Back to square one; back to the daily routine

א לעבן אויף זיין קאפ
A leben oyf zayn kop
TRANSLATION AND MEANING: A blessing on his head

אנגעפאטשקעט
Ongepatshket
TRANSLATION AND MEANING: Overly elaborate; excessively decorated

אזא אויסשטעלער
Aza oysshteler
TRANSLATION AND MEANING: Such a showoff; braggart; egotist

אז מען מוז קען מען
Az men muz ken men
TRANSLATION: If you must, you can
MEANING: You do what you must do

א שאנדע און א חרפה
A shande un a cherpe
TRANSLATION AND MEANING: Shameful and scandalous

אזא שנארער
Aza shnorer
TRANSLATION: Such a moocher
MEANING: A mooch; a cheapskate; a beggar

א חולערע זאל אים טרעפן
A cholere zol im trefn
TRANSLATION: He should encounter a cholera
MEANING: A plague on him

א מיידל מיט אן אויערינגל
A meydl mit an oyeringl
TRANSLATION: A girl with an earring
MEANING: A girl who will go after what she wants regardless of how she gets it, or who she hurts

א גליק האט דיך געטראפן
A glik hot dich getrofn
TRANSLATION: You encountered happiness
MEANING: Big deal (meant sarcastically)

אלץ מיט א צו איז אומגעזונט
Alts mit a tsu iz umgezunt
TRANSLATION: Everything with a 'too' is unhealthy
MEANING: Too much of anything is unhealthy

איך זאל אזוי וויסן פון צרות
Ich zol azoy visn fun tsores
TRANSLATION: I should know as little about trouble as I know about what you are asking me
MEANING: I haven't the faintest idea!

א ברירה האב איך?
A breyreh hob ich?

TRANSLATION AND MEANING: Do I have a choice?

אז א יאר אויף מיר
Az a yor oyf mir
TRANSLATION: Like a year on me
MEANING: I should have such luck

איך דארף דאס ווי א לאך אין קאפ
Ich darf dos vi a loch in kop
TRANSLATION: I need this like a hole in the head
MEANING: I don't need it

איך ארבעט ווי א פערד
Ich arbet vi a ferd
TRANSLATION: I'm working like a horse
MEANING: I'm working really hard

איך גיי חלש'ן באלט אוועק
Ich gey chaleshen balt avek
TRANSLATION: I will soon faint
MEANING:

Used to describe feeling of shock or exhaustion

איך יאג זיך נישט
Ich yog zich nisht
TRANSLATION AND MEANING: I'm in no hurry

אז מיר וועלן שלאגן א הונט, געפונט מען א שטעקן
Az mir veln shlogn a hunt, gefunt men a shtekn
TRANSLATION: If one wants to beat a dog, one finds a stick
MEANING: One can always find a reason to beat someone down

אז מען קען נישט אריבער, גייט מען ארונטער
Az men ken nisht ariber, geyt men arunter
TRANSLATION: If you can't go over, you go under
MEANING: If you can't get it the way you want it, you have to settle for less

אז מיר זוכט, געפונט מען
Az mir zucht, gefunt men
TRANSLATION AND MEANING: If you search, you will find

אז מען דארף דעם גנב, שנייד מען אים אראפ פון דער תליה
Az men darf dem ganev, shnayd men im arop fun der tliye
TRANSLATION: When you need the thief, you cut him down from the gallows
MEANING: When you need someone's help, even if you find him very distasteful, you hold your nose and avail yourself of his service

אזוינס און אזעלעכס
Azoyns un azelechs
TRANSLATION: Such a thing and such a thing
MEANING: A fabulous thing/person

אייזענעם קאפ
Ayzenem kop
TRANSLATION: Head of steel
MEANING: Brilliant

א גראבער יונג
A grober yung
TRANSLATION: A fat, uncouth man
MEANING: An ignoramus

אין א שיינעם עפל געפונט מען א מאל א ווארעם
In a sheynem epl gefunt men a mol a vorem
TRANSLATION: In a beautiful apple you sometimes find a worm
MEANING: Appearances can be deceiving

אלע שוסטערס גייען בארוועס
Ale shusters geyen borves
TRANSLATION: All shoemakers go barefoot
MEANING: People often neglect those closest to them

א בער לערנט מען אויך אויס טאנצן
A ber lernt men oych oys tantsn
TRANSLATION: Even a bear can be taught to dance
MEANING: You can teach anything to anybody

אויב די באבע וואלט געהאט א בארד, וואלט זי געווען א זיידע
Oyb di bubbe volt gehat a bord, volt zi geven a zeide
TRANSLATION: If the grandma had a beard, she would be a grandpa
MEANING: It's pointless to speculate about something you can't change

אויב די באבע וואלט געהאט רעדער, וואלט זי געווען א וואגן
Oyb di bubbe volt gehat reder, volt zi geven a vogn

TRANSLATION:
If the grandma had wheels, she would be a wagon
MEANING:
It's pointless to speculate about something you can't change

••••••••••

אז דאס מיידל קען נישט טאנצן, זאגט זי אז די קלעזמער קענען נישט שפילן

Az dos meydl ken nisht tantsn, zogt zi az di klezmer kenen nisht shpiln

TRANSLATION:
If the girl can't dance, she says the musicians don't know how to play
MEANING:
Laying the blame on someone else for your inability to do something; a bad workman blames his tools

••••••••••

אז מען עסט חזיר, זאל עס שוין רינען איבערן מויל

Az men est chazer, zol es shoyn rinen ibern moyl

TRANSLATION:
If you're going to eat pork, let it drip from your mouth
MEANING:
If you are going to sin, enjoy it to the fullest

••••••••••

אז מען שלאפט מיט הינט, שטייט מען אויף מיט פליי

Az men shloft mit hint, shteyt men oyf mit fley

TRANSLATION:
If you sleep with dogs, you get up with fleas
MEANING:
If you associate with bad people, you will acquire their undesirable traits; be cautious of the company you keep

••••••••••

א מאל איז די רפואה ערגער ווי די מכה

Amol is di refuah erger vi di makeh

TRANSLATION AND MEANING:
Sometimes the cure is worse than the disease

••••••••••

איינעמען זאל ער א מיתה-משונה

Aynnemen zol er a mise-meshune

TRANSLATION AND MEANING:
He should die a violent death

••••••••••

א גאנץ יאר שיכור און פורים ניכטער

A gants yor shiker un Purim nichter

TRANSLATION:
Drunk the whole year and sober on Purim
MEANING:
Does everything backwards

••••••••••

א שיינע ריינע כפרה

A sheyne reyne kapore

TRANSLATION:
A handsome, pure rooster, slaughtered for the atonement ritual on the eve of *Yom Kippur*
MEANING:
Good riddance

••••••••••

א גאנצע קנאקער

A gantse knaker

TRANSLATION:
A whole doorknocker
MEANING:
A big showoff

••••••••••

איך האב אים אין דער לינקער פאה

Ich hob im in der linker peyeh

TRANSLATION:
I have him in the left sidelock
MEANING:
I couldn't care less about him

••••••••••

אז מען גיסט סמאלע אויפן קאפ, פארגעסט מען פון ציינווייטיק

Az men gist smole oyfn kop, fargest men fun tseynveytik

TRANSLATION:
When tar is poured on your head, you forget about your toothache
MEANING:
When bad things happen to you, you forget about your minor problems

••••••••••

אז מען שמירט, פארט מען

Az men shmirt, fort men

TRANSLATION:

If you grease, you travel well
MEANING: When you bribe someone, everything goes well; to grease someone's palm

ביטער ווי גאַל
Biter vi gol
TRANSLATION: Bitter like bile
MEANING: Very bitter

ביליג איז טייער
Bilig iz tayer
TRANSLATION: Cheap is expensive
MEANING: It ends up costing you more when you buy something cheap

ביליג ווי באָרשט
Bilig vi borsht
TRANSLATION: Cheap as borscht (soup made with beetroot)
MEANING: Ridiculously cheap

בעסער צו פֿאַרלירן מיט אַ חכם ווי איידער צו געווינען מיט אַ נאַר
Beser tsu farlirn mit a chochem vi eyder tsu gevinen mit a nar
TRANSLATION: Better to lose to a sage (smart person) than to win with a fool
MEANING: Deal with a smart person, not a fool

בעסער אַ פּאַטש פֿון אַ קלוגער ווי איידער אַ קוש פֿון אַ נאַר
Beser a patsh fun a kluger vi eyder a kush fun a nar
TRANSLATION: Better a slap from a wise person than a kiss from a fool
MEANING: It's better to deal with a smart person than a fool

בלוט איז דיקער ווי וואַסער
Blut iz diker vi vaser
TRANSLATION: Blood is thicker than water
MEANING: Family relationships and loyalties are the strongest and most important ones

בעסער צו האָבן נחת פֿון דער ווײַטן ווי איידער צו האָבן צרות פֿון דער נאָענט
Beser tsu hobn nachas fun der vaytn vi eyder tsu hobn tsores fun der noent
TRANSLATION AND MEANING: Better to have joy from afar than troubles from close

באַנק קוועטשער
Bonk kvetcher
TRANSLATION: A bench squeezer
MEANING: Someone who sits and learns Torah but doesn't take it seriously

גוט מאָרגען געלע, רייטאַך טראָג איך
Gut morgen Gele, reytach trog ich
TRANSLATION: Good morning Gelle, I'm carrying radishes
MEANING: One word or thought has nothing to do with the other

גרויסער צולייגער
Groyser tsuleyger
TRANSLATION: Big explainer
MEANING: Big talker

גם זו לטובה
Gam zu letovah
TRANSLATION: This is a Hebrew phrase: This, too, is for the best
MEANING: Although not obvious, this occurrence is for a good reason; resembles English aphorism "every cloud has a silver lining"

גיי מאָל אויס אַ בלינדן רויט
Gey mol oys a blindn royt
TRANSLATION: Go describe (the color) red to a blind person
MEANING: You can never explain something

to someone who hasn't experienced it

גיי קלאפ דיין קאפ אין דער וואנט
Gey clop dayn kop in der vant
TRANSLATION: Go bang your head in the wall
MEANING: Get lost!

גאט זיצט פון אויבן און פארט פון אונטן
Got zitst fun oyvn un purt fun untn
TRANSLATION: God sits above and pairs (people) below
MEANING: Matches are made in heaven

גאט שיקט די רפואה פאר דער מכה
Got shikt di refuah far der makeh
TRANSLATION: God sends the remedy before the illness
MEANING: The solution became available before the problem occurred

די וואנט האבן אויערן
Di vent hobn oyern
TRANSLATION: Walls have ears
MEANING: Be careful what you say as people may be eavesdropping

די נאר שטופט דיך
Di nar shtupt dich
TRANSLATION: The fool is pushing you.
MEANING: Your own stupidities are causing you to act foolish. Your foolishness is coming out

די נשמה אין די הענט
Di neshomah in di hent
TRANSLATION: The soul in the hands
MEANING: Very scared

דו ביסט א זא אנטשעפעניש
Du bist a za ontshepenish
TRANSLATION: You are such a cling on
MEANING: You are such a pest, a nuisance

דער אמת שווימט ארויף ווי בוימל אויפן וואסער
Der emes shvimt aroyf vi boyml oyfn vaser
TRANSLATION: The truth swims up like oil on top of water
MEANING: The truth comes out

די גאנצע וועלט איז איין שטעטל
Di gantse velt iz eyn shtetl
TRANSLATION: The whole world is one village
MEANING: It's a small world

דער עולם איז א גולם
Der oylem iz a goylem
TRANSLATION: The world is a fool
MEANING: The masses are fools; expression used to challenge public opinion

דאס עפעלע פאלט נישט ווייט פון בוים
Dos epele falt nisht vayt fun boym
TRANSLATION AND MEANING: The apple doesn't fall far from the tree

דער שכל איז א קריכער
Der seychel iz a kricher
TRANSLATION AND MEANING: Common sense, understanding, come at a snail's pace

דער מענטש טראכט און גאט לאכט
Der mentsh tracht un Got lacht
TRANSLATION: Man plans, and God laughs
MEANING: Man's best laid plans can be overturned at any moment

דער קאפ זאל אים אראפ
Der kop zol im

arop
TRANSLATION AND MEANING: His head should fall off; this is used as a curse

דער ריינע אמת איז דער בעסטער ליגנט
Der reyne emes iz der bester lignt
TRANSLATION: The clean truth is the best lie
MEANING: It's better to come clean, to tell the truth

האבן אין באָרד
Hobn in bord
TRANSLATION: To have in the beard
MEANING: To not care about someone

האניג אויפן צונג, גאל אויפן לונג
Honig oyfn tsung, gal oyfn lung
TRANSLATION: Honey on the tongue, bile on the lung
MEANING: Talks nicely but doesn't mean it; two faced

וואו קומט די קאץ איבערן וואסער?
Vu kumpt di kats ibern vaser?
TRANSLATION: How does the cat cross the water?
MEANING: How do we accomplish such a difficult task?

וואו א נאר אויפן מארק
Vu a nar oyfn mark
TRANSLATION: Like a fool in the marketplace
MEANING: Like a fool

וואו פון די לבנה אראפ
Vu fun di levahna arup
TRANSLATION: As if from the moon
MEANING: Strange; weird; bizarre

ווען א נאר ווארפט א שטיין אריין אין וואסער, קענען נישט קיין צען קלוגע עס ארויסנעמען
Ven a nar varft a shteyn arayn in vaser, kenen nisht kayn tsen kluge es aroysnemen

ווען די נאר איז נישט מיינער, וואלט איך אויך געלאכט
Ven di nar is nisht mayner volt ich oych gelacht
TRANSLATION: If the fool wasn't mine, I would also laugh
MEANING: It isn't funny (for me) when the fool belongs to me

ווען יוסל וויל טאנצן, גייען די מיוזיקאנטן פישן
Ven Yosl vil tantsn, geyen di muzikantn pishn
TRANSLATION: When Yossel wants to dance, the musicians go pee
MEANING: By the time he gets his act together, he missed the opportunity; the ship has sailed

TRANSLATION: When a fool throws a stone into the water, even ten wise men can't get it out
MEANING: You can't easily undo something a fool does

וואו איינער איז צו זיבן, אזוי איז ער צו זיבעציג
Vu eyner iz tsu zibn, azoy iz er tsu zibetsig
TRANSLATION: As one is at seven, so is he at seventy
MEANING: A person never changes; a leopard doesn't change its spots

וואו מיר בעט זיך, אזוי שלאפט מען
Vu mir bet zich, azoy shloft men
TRANSLATION: The way you make your bed is the way you sleep
MEANING: You suffer the consequences of your actions

Mom's Yiddish Idioms

וואס לויפסטו? עס ברענט נישט!

Vos loyfstu? Es brent nisht!

TRANSLATION: Why are you running? It's not burning!

MEANING: What's your hurry? Don't get excited!

....

ווייז א חזיר א פינגער, וויל ער די גאנצע האנט

Vayz a chazer a finger, vil er di gantse hant

TRANSLATION: Show a pig a finger and he'll want the whole hand

MEANING: Make a small concession and they will take advantage of you; give an inch and they'll take a mile

....

ווען די קאץ שלאפט, טאנצן די מייז

Ven di kats shloft, tantsn di mayz

TRANSLATION: When the cat's asleep, the mice dance

MEANING: When the person in charge is not present, the subordinates do as they please; when the cat's away the mice will play

....

ווען מיר גיט א קלאפ אין טיש, רופט זיך אן די שער

Ven mir git a clop in tish, ruft zich on di sher

TRANSLATION: When you bang on the table, the scissors respond

MEANING: Said to a person who interrupts a conversation with unsolicited input

....

זינגען ווי א פויגל

Zingen vi a foygl

TRANSLATION: Sing like a bird

MEANING: To admit to the truth; to come clean

....

זי איז א זא בעריער

Zi iz a za beriyer

TRANSLATION AND MEANING: She is very capable

....

זי האט זיך אנגעטאן ווי יענטעלע צום געט

Zi hot zich ongeton vui Yentele tsum get

TRANSLATION: She got herself dressed up like Yentele going for a Jewish divorce

MEANING: She's so overdressed

....

זי איז א זא צאצקע

Zi is a za tsatske

TRANSLATION AND MEANING: She is such a piece of work

....

זי וויל דאס טעלערל פון הימל

Zi vil dos telerl fun himl

TRANSLATION: She wants the plate from the sky

MEANING: She wants the moon; she's very demanding

....

חכם פון די מה נשתנה

Chocham fun di Ma Nishtana

TRANSLATION: Wise man from the Ma Nishtana of the Passover Haggadah

MEANING: A fool

....

טויג אויף כפרות

Toyg oyf Kapores

TRANSLATION: Good for the atonement ritual of Kaparot performed on the eve of *Yom Kippur*

MEANING: Worthless; good for nothing

....

טו אן א חזיר א שטריימל, וועט ער ווערן רב?

Tu on a chazir a shtreimel, vet er vern rov?

TRANSLATION: If you put a shtreimel on a pig, would it make him a rabbi?

MEANING: You can't dress someone up to be someone he is not

יעדן
מאנטיק און
דאנערשטאג
Yedn Montik un donershtug
TRANSLATION:
Every Monday and Thursday
MEANING:
Often

יענער פויגל
Yener foygl
TRANSLATION:
That bird
MEANING:
A real troublemaker

יענעם'ס צרות
לאזן שלאפן
Yenem's tsores lozn shlofn
TRANSLATION:
Someone else's troubles let you sleep
MEANING:
You are not so affected by someone else's troubles

יעדער מענטש
האט זיך זיין
פעקל
Yeder mentsh hot zich zayn pekl
TRANSLATION:
Every person has his own bundle
MEANING:
Everyone has his own burden

יעדער מענטש
האט זיך
זיין אייגענע
משוגעת
Yeder mentsh hot zich zayn eygene meshugas
TRANSLATION:
Each person has his own craziness
MEANING:
Everyone is crazy in their own way

יעדער טעפל
האט א דעקל
Yeder tepl hot a dekl
TRANSLATION:
Every pot has a lid
MEANING:
There's someone for everyone

כאפן א דרימל
Chapn a driml
TRANSLATION:
Catch a nap
MEANING:
Take a nap

כאפן הייסע
לאקשן
Chapn heyse lokshen
TRANSLATION:
Catching hot noodles
MEANING:
Hastily approaching something

לאכן זאל
ער מיט
יאשטשערקעס
Lachn zol er mit yashtsherkes
TRANSLATION:
He should laugh with lizards
MEANING:
He should laugh out of bitterness rather than joy or to laugh on the outside while crying on the inside

מיט אלע
פיטשיווקעס
Mit ale pitchivkes
TRANSLATION:
With all the trinkets
MEANING:
With all the trimmings

מיאס ווי די
נאכט
Mies vi di nacht
TRANSLATION:
As ugly as the night
MEANING:
Very ugly

מאך זיך נישט
וויסנדיג
Mach zich nisht visndig
TRANSLATION:
Act as though you don't know
MEANING:
Ignore it

מיין באבע'ס
טעם
Mayn bubbe's tam
TRANSLATION:
My grandma's taste
MEANING:
It's tasteless

משה קאפאיער
Moishe kapoyer
TRANSLATION:
Moshe backwards
MEANING:
All mixed up, backwards; said when things don't go smoothly

מען ווארפט
נישט ארויס
אומריינע
וואסער איידער
מען האט ריינע
Men varft nisht aroys umreyne vaser eyder men hot reyne
TRANSLATION:

We don't throw out the dirty water before we have clean water
MEANING: We shouldn't throw something out before we have a replacement for it

⋯⋯⋯⋯⋯

מיש זיך נישט אריין
Mish zich nisht arayn
TRANSLATION: Don't mix in
MEANING: Mind your own business

מ'לייגט נישט א געזונטן קאפ אין א קראנקן בעט
M'leygt nisht a gezuntn kop in a krankn bet
TRANSLATION: One shouldn't put a healthy head into a sick bed
MEANING: One should knowingly not put oneself into a dangerous situation or into a situation in which it is impossible to succeed

⋯⋯⋯⋯⋯

מיט איין תחת קען מען נישט טאנצן אויף צוויי חתונות
Mit eyn toches ken men nisht tantsn oyf tsvey chasenes
TRANSLATION: You can't dance at two weddings with one behind
MEANING: You can't be in two places at one time

מיר וועלן שיסן צוויי האזן מיט איין שאס
Mir veln shisn tsvey hozn mit eyn shos
TRANSLATION: We'll shoot two rabbits with one shot
MEANING: We'll achieve two objectives with one action; we'll kill two birds with one stone.

⋯⋯⋯⋯⋯

מיט האניג קען מען כאפן מער פליגן ווי מיט עסיג
Mit honig ken men chapn mer flign vi mit esig
TRANSLATION: You can catch more flies with honey than with vinegar
MEANING: It's easier to persuade others with polite requests than with ill-mannered demands

⋯⋯⋯⋯⋯

מען שיקט נישט א קאץ נאך סמעטענע
Men shikt nisht a kats noch smetene
TRANSLATION: You don't send a cat for sour cream
MEANING: Don't send someone for something you know they want or need, because they will take it for themselves

⋯⋯⋯⋯⋯

נישט אלעס וואס גלאנצט איז גאלד
Nisht ales vos glantst is gold
TRANSLATION AND MEANING: Not everything that shines is golden

⋯⋯⋯⋯⋯

נישט אריין טון קיין פינגער אין קאלטע וואסער
Nisht arayn tun kayn finger in kalte vaser
TRANSLATION: Won't put a finger into cold water
MEANING: Won't do a thing; lazy; won't lift a finger

⋯⋯⋯⋯⋯

נישט געשטויגן נישט געפלויגן
Nisht geshtoygn nisht gefloygn
TRANSLATION: It never rose, it never flew
MEANING: It never happened; said in response to a dubious or far-fetched story

⋯⋯⋯⋯⋯

נעם די אויגן אין די הענט
Nem di oygn in di hent
TRANSLATION: Take your eyes in your hands
MEANING: Be careful; watch out

⋯⋯⋯⋯⋯

ס'קומט אן מיט גרינע ווארעם
S'kumt un mit grine vorem
TRANSLATION: It comes on like green worms

MEANING:
It is exceedingly difficult

ס'איז א חסרון אז די כלה איז צו שיין
Siz a chasoren az di kallah iz tsu sheyn
TRANSLATION:
It's a drawback that the bride is too pretty
MEANING:
The fault finder will even complain that the bride is too pretty, i.e., will complain about everything

עס טוט זיך אויף טיש און אויף בענק
Es tut zich oyf tish un oyf benk
TRANSLATION:
Things are happening on tables and chairs
MEANING:
A hullabaloo

ער איז אראפ פון זינען
Er iz arup fun zinen
TRANSLATION AND MEANING:
He is out of his mind

ער איז א זא פראסטאק
Er iz a za prostak
TRANSLATION AND MEANING:
He is such an ignorant, vulgar person

ער איז פארבלאנדזעט געווארן
Er iz farblondzhet gevorn
TRANSLATION:
He got lost
MEANING:
He's lost or he's all mixed up

ער איז גאט'ס גנב
Er iz Got's ganev
TRANSLATION:
He is God's thief
MEANING:
He acts innocently and piously but in reality he is neither.

ער איז גאט די נשמה שולדיג
Er iz Got di neshoma shuldig
TRANSLATION:
He owes God his soul

MEANING:
He owes everybody money

עס ווערט מיר פינסטער פאר די אויגן
Es vert mir finster far di oygn
TRANSLATION:
It's getting dark before my eyes
MEANING:
I'm fainting! (in response to receiving bad news); things are looking bad

עס וועט זיך אלץ אויספרעסין
Es vet zich alts oyspresin
TRANSLATION:
It will all iron itself out.
MEANING:
It will all work out

ער איז א שטיק פלייש מיט צוויי אויגן
Er iz a shtik fleysh mit tsvey oygn
TRANSLATION:
He is piece of meat with two eyes

MEANING:
He's really stupid

ער קען קיין צוויי נישט ציילן
Er ken kayn tsvey nisht tseyln
TRANSLATION:
He can't count to two
MEANING:
He's really stupid

ער האט א קאץ אין קאפ
Er hot a kats in kop
TRANSLATION:
He has a cat in his head
MEANING:
He's really stupid

עס קלעבט זיך נישט א ווארט צו א ווארט
Es klept zich nisht a vort tsu a vort
TRANSLATION:
One word doesn't stick to another
MEANING:
He speaks very unintelligently; he doesn't make sense

עס שיטן זיך פערל פון זיין מויל

Es shitn zich perl fun zayn moyl

TRANSLATION: Pearls flow from his mouth

MEANING: Pearls of wisdom flow from his mouth; he speaks eloquently

....

עס וועט העלפן ווי א טויטן באנקעס

Es vet helfn vi a toytn bonkes

TRANSLATION AND MEANING: It's as helpful as fire cupping (a medical remedy) a corpse

....

ער האט שפילקעס אין תחת

Er hot shpilkes in toches

TRANSLATION: He has pins in his behind

MEANING: He's very restless

....

עס פאסט ווי א חזיר א שטריימל

Es past vi a chazer a shtreimel

TRANSLATION: It's as fitting as a shtreimel on a pig

MEANING: It's not suitable

....

ער מאכט וואסער אויף קאשע

Er macht vaser oyf kasha

TRANSLATION: He earns water on kasha (buckwheat)

MEANING: He earns very little money

....

ער וואלט פארקויפט זיין מאמע מיט זיין טאטע

Er volt farkoyft zayn momme mit zayn tatte

TRANSLATION: He would sell his mother and father

MEANING: He would do anything for money

....

ער טשעפעט זיך אין די נאסע וועגט

Er tshepet zich in di nase vent

TRANSLATION: He disturbs/bothers the wet walls

MEANING: He's in a bad mood, and for no good reason, is looking for an argument or fight

....

ער רעדט פאר פייער און פאר וואסער

Er redt far fayer un far vaser

TRANSLATION: He talks for fire and for water

MEANING: He's a blabbermouth

....

פארדריי מיר נישט קיין קאפ

Fardrey mir nisht kayn kop

TRANSLATION: Don't spin my head

MEANING: Don't make me crazy. Leave me alone

....

פון א חזר'ישן עק קען מען קיין שטריימל נישט מאכן

Fun a chazer'ishn ek ken men kayn shtreimel nisht machn

TRANSLATION: You can't make a shtreimel out of a pig's tail

MEANING: You can't produce something refined, admirable or valuable from something which is unrefined, unpleasant or of little or no value; in the case of people, you can't turn a boor into a refined person

....

פויפסטלעכער ווי די פויפ

Poypstlecher vi di poyp

TRANSLATION: More Pope-like than the Pope

MEANING: Holier than thou; someone with an air of superior morality or piety

....

צו באַרשט דארף מען נישט קיין ציין

Tsu borsht darf men nisht kayn tseyn

TRANSLATION: You don't need teeth to eat borscht

MEANING:
It's obvious

צוריק גייט א קאזע
Tsurik geyt a koze
TRANSLATION:
Back goes a goat
MEANING:
You can't take it back; you can't undo what you did; once you give it away, you won't get it back.

קום ווי ער זשיפיט
Koiym vi er zhipit
TRANSLATION:
He's barely breathing
MEANING:
He's on his last leg

קליינע קינדער לאזן נישט שלאפן, גרויסע קינדער לאזן נישט לעבן
Kleyne kinder lozn nisht shlofn, groyse kinder lozn nisht leben
TRANSLATION AND MEANING:
Little children don't let you sleep, older children don't let you live

קליינע קינדער קליינע צרות, גרויסע קינדער גרויסע צרות
Kleyne kinder kleyne tsores, groyse kinder groyse tsores
TRANSLATION AND MEANING:
Little children little problems, big children big problems

קיינער זעט נישט זיין אייגענעם הויקער
Keyner zet nisht zayn eygenem hoyker
TRANSLATION:
No one sees the hump on his own back
MEANING:
No one sees his/her own flaws

קיינער ווייסט נישט וועמען דער שוך קוועטשט נאר דער וואס גייט אין אים
Keyner veyst nisht vemen der shuch kvetsht nor der vos geyt in im
TRANSLATION:
No one knows whose shoe pinches except the person who walks in it
MEANING:
Nobody can fully understand another person's hardship or suffering.

רויט ווי א באריק
Royt vi a barik
TRANSLATION:
Red like a beet
MEANING:
Red faced, embarrassed

שלאג מיך נישט און לעק מיך נישט
Shlog mich nisht un lek mich nisht
TRANSLATION:
Don't hit me and don't lick me
MEANING:
Don't be nasty to me and then be nice to me

שטיל וואסער גראבט טיף
Shtil vaser grobt tif
TRANSLATION:
Still water digs (runs) deep
MEANING:
People who are quiet and shy may often be intelligent, interesting, and passionate

APPENDIX III

The Budniewski Family

My mother never saw the Budniewskis again after they left Poland for the Ukraine in 1944, although she kept in touch with them her entire life. She often spoke about their unparalleled generosity and heroism, and the immense debt of gratitude owed to them.

Matvey (Matewka) Antonovich Budniewski:
Born November 28, 1908, in Horodlo, Poland; died November 18, 1968, in Volodymyr-Volynsky, Ukraine.

Yekaterina (Katya) Antonovna Budniewska:
Born June 4, 1910, in Horodlo, Poland; died October 23, 1983, in Volodymyr-Volynsky, Ukraine.

Liya Budniewska (daughter):
Born August 6, 1943, in Horodlo, Poland; died December 13, 2014. Volodymyr-Volynsky, Ukraine.
Son: Matvey (Mitja) Budniewski, born July 12, 1980, in Volodymyr-Volynsky, Ukraine.

Galik Matveyevich Budniewski (son):
Born October 13, 1947; died July 6, 2009, in Volodymyr-Volynsky, Ukraine. Married Lidija. Children: Anton Budniewski, born 1984, and Liudmilla Budniewska, born 1985. Volodymyr – Volynsky, Ukraine.

Liya's son, Matvey holding his grandparents'
Righteous Among the Nations Certificate. Ukraine, 2021.

APPENDIX IV

Family Tree

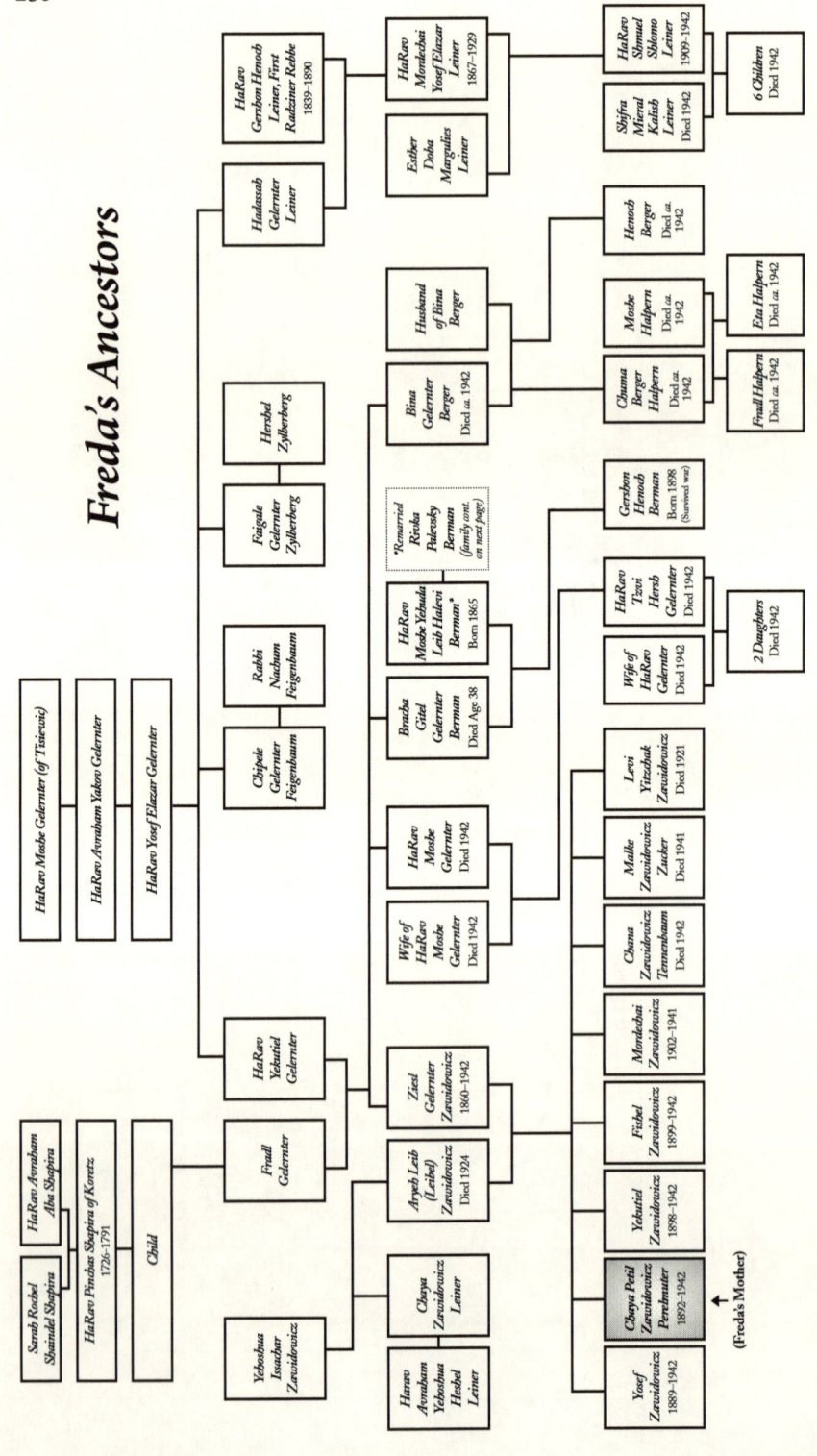

Freda's Ancestors

- Sarah Rochel Shaindel Shapira
- HaRav Avraham Aba Shapira
- HaRav Pinchas Shapira of Korretz, 1726–1791
- Child
- HaRav Moshe Gelernter (of Tisievcic)
- HaRav Avraham Yakov Gelernter
- HaRav Yosef/Elazar Gelernter

- Yehoshua Issachar Zwuidowicz
- Fraidl Gelernter
- HaRav Yehutiel Gelernter
- Chipele Gelernter Feigenbaum
- Rabbi Nachum Feigenbaum
- Faigale Gelernter Zylberberg
- Hershel Zylberberg
- Hadassah Gelernter Leiner
- HaRav Gershon Henoch Leiner, First Radziner Rebbe, 1839–1890

- HaRav Avraham Yehoshua Heshel Leiner
- Chaya Zwuidowicz Leiner
- Aryeh Leib (Leibel) Zwuidowicz Died 1924
- Ziesl Gelernter Zwuidowicz 1860–1942
- Wife of HaRav Moshe Gelernter Died 1942
- HaRav Moshe Gelernter Died 1942
- Bracha Gitel Gelernter Berman Died Age 38
- HaRav Moshe Yehuda Leib Halevi Berman* Born 1865
- *Remarried Rivka Pulevsky Berman (family cont. on next page)
- Bina Gelernter Berger Died ca. 1942
- Husband of Bina Berger
- HaRav Mordechai Yosef/Elazar Leiner 1867–1929
- Esther Doba Margulies Leiner

- Henoch Berger Died ca. 1942
- HaRav Shmuel Shlomo Leiner 1909–1942
- Shifra Mieral Kalizb Leiner Died 1942
- 6 Children Died 1942

- Yosef Zwuidowicz 1889–1942
- Chaya Peril Zwuidowicz Perelmuter 1892–1942 ← (Freda's Mother)
- Yekutiel Zwuidowicz 1898–1942
- Fishel Zwuidowicz 1899–1942
- Mordechai Zwuidowicz 1902–1941
- Chana Zwuidowicz Tennenbaum Died 1942
- Malke Zwuidowicz Zucker Died 1941
- Levi Yitzchak Zwuidowicz Died 1921
- Wife of HaRav Tzvi Hersh Gelernter Died 1942
- HaRav Tzvi Hersh Gelernter Died 1942
- Gershon Henoch Berman Born 1898 (Survived war)
- 2 Daughters Died 1942
- Chana Berger Halpern
- Moshe Halpern Died ca. 1942
- Fraidl Halpern Died ca. 1942
- Eta Halpern Died ca. 1942

Family of HaRav Moshe Yehuda Halevi & Rivka Berman

(Continued from previous page)

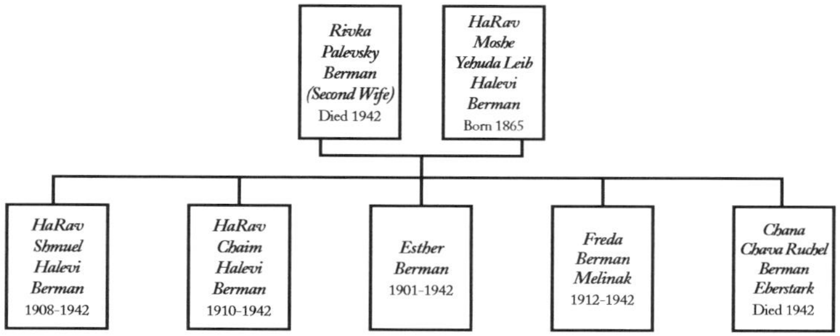

```
                    ┌─────────────────┬─────────────────┐
                    │ Rivka           │ HaRav Moshe     │
                    │ Paltevsky       │ Yehuda Leib     │
                    │ Berman          │ Halevi          │
                    │ (Second Wife)   │ Berman          │
                    │ Died 1942       │ Born 1865       │
                    └─────────────────┴─────────────────┘
                                    │
    ┌───────────────┬───────────────┼───────────────┬───────────────┐
┌─────────┐   ┌─────────┐     ┌─────────┐     ┌─────────┐     ┌─────────┐
│ HaRav   │   │ HaRav   │     │ Esther  │     │ Freda   │     │ Chana   │
│ Shmuel  │   │ Chaim   │     │ Berman  │     │ Berman  │     │ Chava Rueb│
│ Halevi  │   │ Halevi  │     │ 1901-1942│    │ Melinak │     │ Berman  │
│ Berman  │   │ Berman  │     │         │    │ 1912-1942│    │ Eberstark│
│ 1908-1942│  │ 1910-1942│    │         │    │         │     │ Died 1942│
└─────────┘   └─────────┘     └─────────┘     └─────────┘     └─────────┘
```

237

The Radziner Relation

Note: Freda's great-grandfather's sister, Hadassah, was married to the first Radziner Rebbe, HaRav Gershon Henoch Leiner. Freda's grandfather's sister, Chaya, was married to HaRav Avraham Yehoshua Heshel Leiner, the brother of HaRav Gershon Henoch Leiner.

*Sister of Freda's grandfather, Aryeh Leib (Leibel) Zavuidovicz.

- HaRav Moshe Gelernter (of Tisevcic)
  - HaRav Avraham Yaakov Gelernter
    - HaRav Yosef Elazar Gelernter
      - HaRav Mordechai Yosef Leiner, Izbhitzer Rebbe 1801–1854
        - HaRav Yaakov Leiner, Izbhitzer Rebbe 1828–1878
          - Hadassah Gelernter Leiner
            - HaRav Gershon Henoch Leiner, First Radziner Rebbe 1839–1890
              - HaRav Mordechai Yosef Elazar Leiner, Radziner Rebbe 1873–1929
                - Esther Deba Margulies Leiner
                - HaRav Shmuel Shlomo Leiner, Radziner Rebbe 1909–1942
                  - Shifra Mirel Kalish Leiner Died 1942
                  - 6 Children Died 1942
          - Chaya (Chaitchul) Zavuidovicz Leiner Died 1944
            - HaRav Avraham Yehoshua Heshel Leiner Died 1920
              - HaRav Yeruchem Leiner, Radziner Rebbe Died 1964
                - Rivka Halberstadt Leiner Died 1960
                - HaRav Mordechai Yosef Leiner, Radziner Rebbe 1918–1991
                  - Rose Hoffman Leiner Died 1995
                  - Miriam Bookson Leiner
                  - HaRav Yakov Leiner, Radziner Rebbe Died 2009
                  - Rivka Leiner Feinstein
                  - HaRav Mordechai Aaron Feinstein
                  - Mali Silverberg Leiner
                  - HaRav Moshe Leiner, Radziner Rebbe of Bayit V'gan
      - HaRav Yehutiel Gelernter
        - Fraidl Gelernter
        - Zissel Gelernter Zavuidovicz 1860–1942
          - Aryeh Leib (Leibel) Zavuidovicz* Died 1924
          - Chaya Petil Zavuidovicz Perelmuter 1892–1942
            - Noson Nuta Perelmuter 1897–1979
            - Freda (Fradl) Perelmuter Schipper 1923–2014
              - Menachem Mendel Schipper 1921–2014

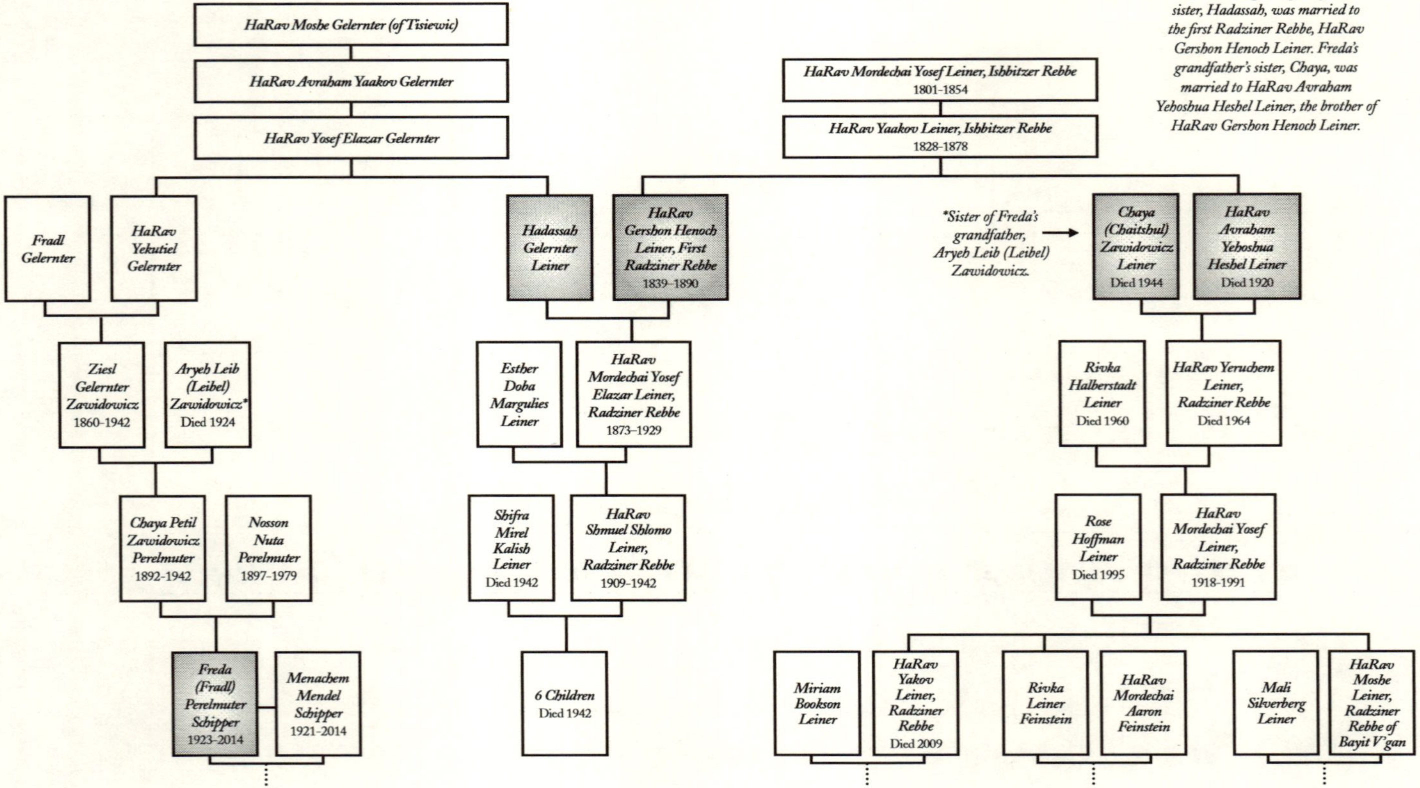

Bubbe Ziesl & Zeide Leibel's Eight Children & Their Families

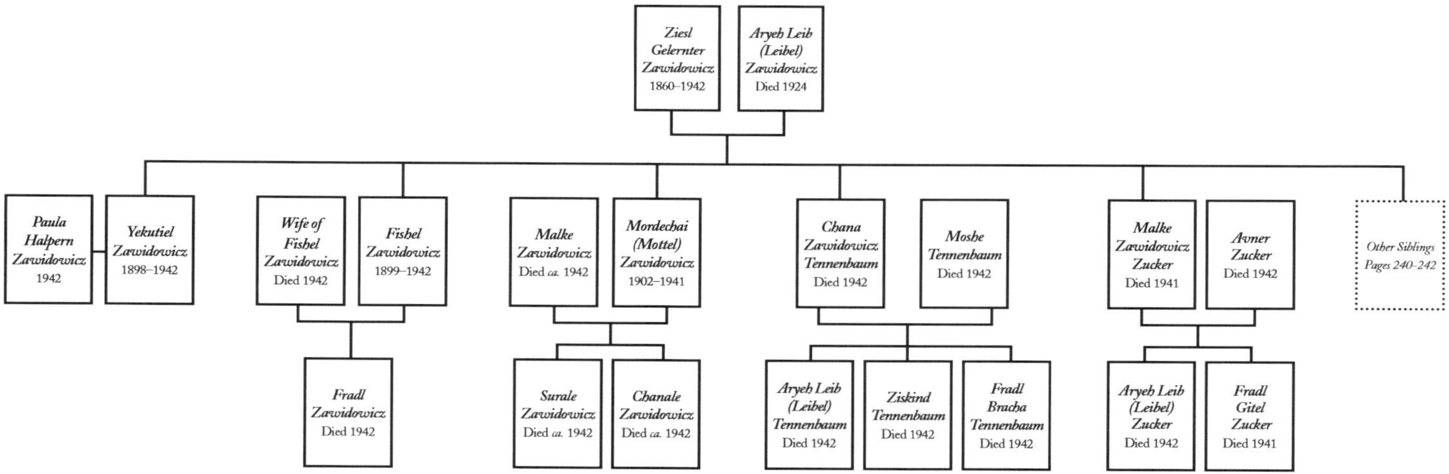

- Ziesl Gelernter Zaruidowicz 1860–1942
- Aryeh Leib (Leibel) Zaruidowicz Died 1924

Children:

Yekutiel Zaruidowicz 1898–1942
- Paula Halpern Zaruidowicz 1942

Fishel Zaruidowicz 1899–1942 & Wife of Fishel Zaruidowicz Died 1942
- Fradl Zaruidowicz Died 1942

Mordechai (Mottel) Zaruidowicz 1902–1941 & Malke Zaruidowicz Died ca. 1942
- Sarule Zaruidowicz Died ca. 1942
- Chanale Zaruidowicz Died ca. 1942

Chana Zaruidowicz Tennenbaum Died 1942 & Moshe Tennenbaum Died 1942
- Aryeh Leib (Leibel) Tennenbaum Died 1942
- Ziskind Tennenbaum Died 1942
- Fradl Brucha Tennenbaum Died 1942

Malke Zaruidowicz Zucker Died 1941 & Asner Zucker Died 1942
- Aryeh Leib (Leibel) Zucker Died 1942
- Fradl Gitel Zucker Died 1941

Other Siblings Pages 240–242

Bubbe Ziesl & Zeide Leibel's Eight Children & Their Families *(Continued)*

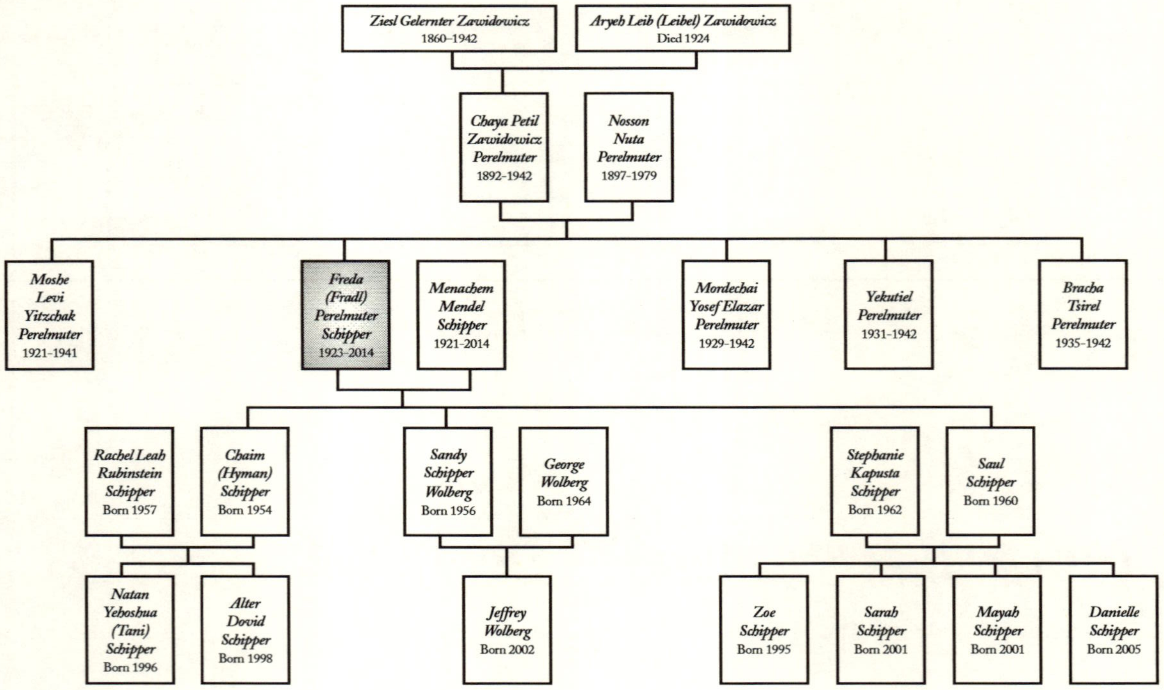

- Ziesl Gelernter Zavulanowicz 1860-1942
- Aryeh Leib (Leibel) Zavulanowicz Died 1924
  - Chaya Peril Zavulanowicz Perelmuter 1892-1942
  - Nosson Nuta Perelmuter 1897-1979
    - Moshe Levi Yitzchak Perelmuter 1921-1941
    - Menachem Mendel Schipper 1921-2014
    - **Freda (Fradl) Perelmuter Schipper 1923-2014**
      - Chaim (Hyman) Schipper Born 1954
        - Rachel Leah Rubinstein Schipper Born 1957
          - Natan Yehoshua (Tani) Schipper Born 1996
          - Alter Dovid Schipper Born 1998
      - Sandy Schipper Wolberg Born 1956
        - George Wolberg Born 1964
          - Jeffrey Wolberg Born 2002
      - Saul Schipper Born 1960
        - Stephanie Kapusta Schipper Born 1962
          - Zoe Schipper Born 1995
          - Sarah Schipper Born 2001
          - Mayah Schipper Born 2001
          - Danielle Schipper Born 2005
    - Mordechai Yosef Elazar Perelmuter 1929-1942
    - Yekutiel Perelmuter 1931-1942
    - Bracha Tsirel Perelmuter 1935-1942

Bubbe Ziesl & Zeide Leibel's Eight Children & Their Families *(Continued)*

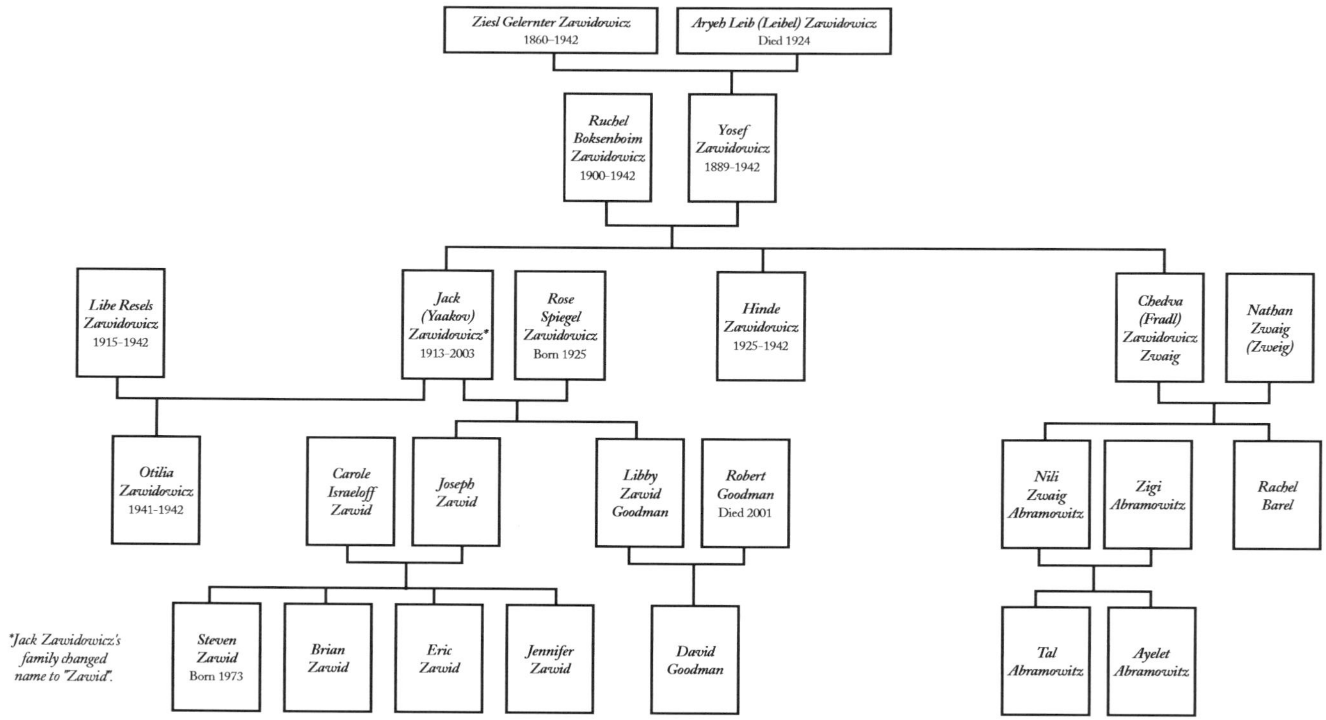

- Ziesl Gelernter Zavuidowicz 1860-1942 — Aryeb Leib (Leibel) Zavuidowicz Died 1924
  - Yosef Zavuidowicz 1889-1942 — Rachel Boksenboim Zavuidowicz 1900-1942
    - Libe Reses Zavuidowicz 1915-1942
      - Ortilia Zavuidowicz 1941-1942
    - Jack (Yaakov) Zavuidowicz* 1913-2003 — Rose Spiegel Zavuidowicz Born 1925
      - Carole Ismaloff Zavuid — Joseph Zavuid
        - Steven Zavuid Born 1973
        - Brian Zavuid
        - Eric Zavuid
        - Jennifer Zavuid
      - Libby Zavuid Goodman — Robert Goodman Died 2001
        - David Goodman
    - Hinde Zavuidowicz 1925-1942
    - Chedva (Fradl) Zavuidowicz Zwaig — Nathan Zwaig (Zweig)
      - Nili Zwaig Abramowitz — Zigi Abramowitz
        - Tal Abramowitz
        - Ayelet Abramowitz
      - Rachel Barel

*Jack Zavuidowicz's family changed name to Zavuid.

Bubbe Ziesl & Zeide Leibel's Eight Children & Their Families *(Continued)*

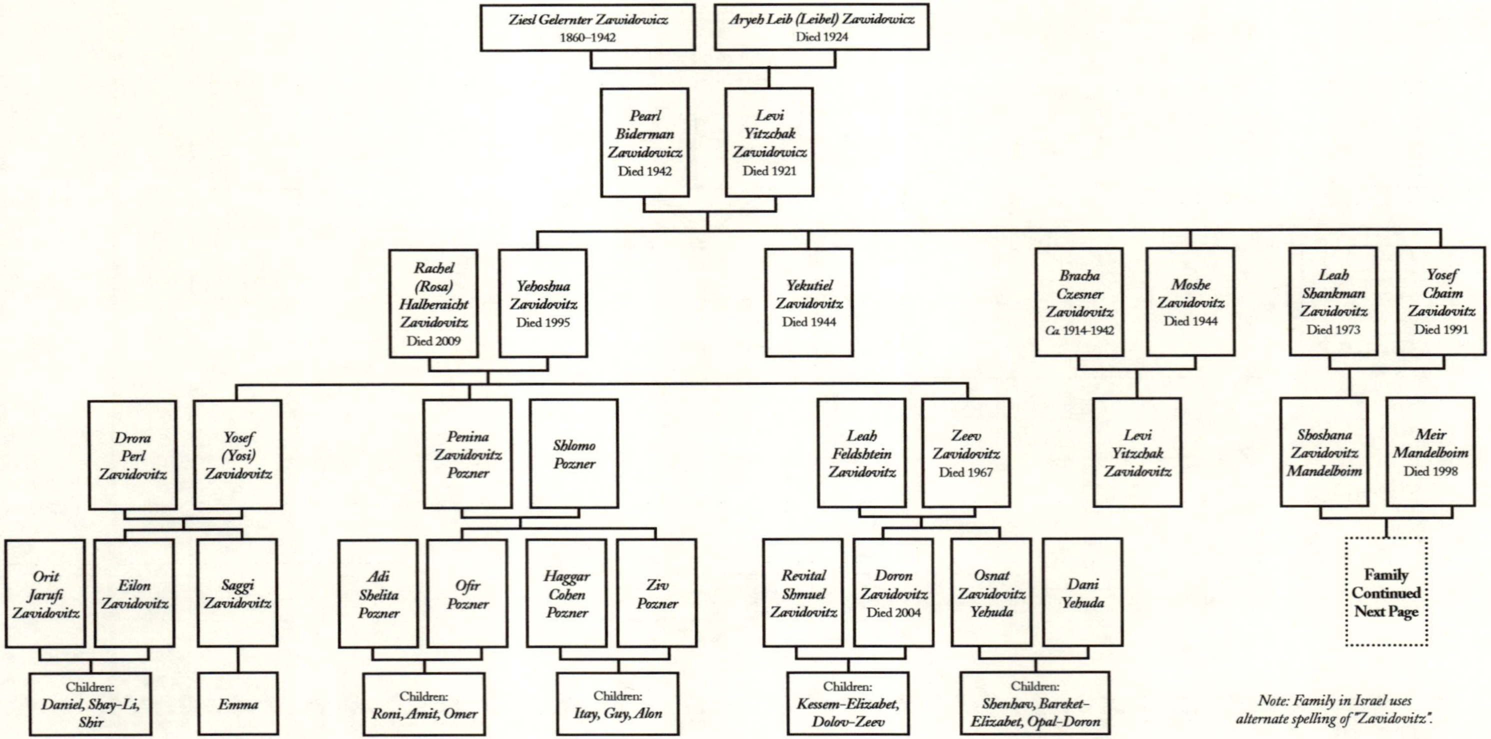

- **Ziesl Gelernter Zaruidovicz** 1860-1942
- **Aryeh Leib (Leibel) Zaruidovicz** Died 1924

Children:
- **Pearl Biderman Zaruidovitz** Died 1942
- **Levi Yitzchak Zaruidovitz** Died 1921

Yekutiel Zaruidovitz — Died 1944
- **Bracha Czesner Zaruidovitz** Ca. 1914-1942
- **Moshe Zaruidovitz** Died 1944
  - *Levi Yitzhak Zaruidovitz*

Leah Shankman Zaruidovitz — Died 1973
- **Yosef Chaim Zaruidovitz** Died 1991
- **Shoshana Zaruidovitz Mandelbeim** / **Meir Mandelbeim** Died 1998
  - Family Continued Next Page

Yehoshua Zaruidovitz — Died 1995
- **Rachel (Rosa) Halbernicht Zaruidovitz** Died 2009

Children:
- **Perina Zaruidovitz Pozner** / **Shlomo Pozner**
  - **Adi Shelta Pozner** / **Ofir Pozner**
    - Children: Roni, Amit, Omer
  - **Haggar Cohen Pozner** / **Ziv Pozner**
    - Children: Itay, Gay, Alon

- **Leah Feldshtein Zaruidovitz** / **Zeev Zaruidovitz** Died 1967
  - **Revital Shmuel Zaruidovitz** / **Doron Zaruidovitz** Died 2004
    - Children: Kessem–Elizabet, Dolev–Zeev
  - **Osnat Zaruidovitz Yehuda** / **Dani Yehuda**
    - Children: Shenhav, Bareket–Elizabet, Opal–Doron

Yosef (Yosi) Zaruidovitz
- **Dvora Perl Zaruidovitz**
- **Orit Jarufi Zaruidovitz**
- **Eilon Zaruidovitz**
  - Children: Daniel, Shay-Li, Shir
- **Saggi Zaruidovitz**
  - *Emma*

Note: Family in Israel uses alternate spelling of "Zaviidovitz".

Family of Shoshana & Meir Mandelboim *(Continued from Previous Page)*

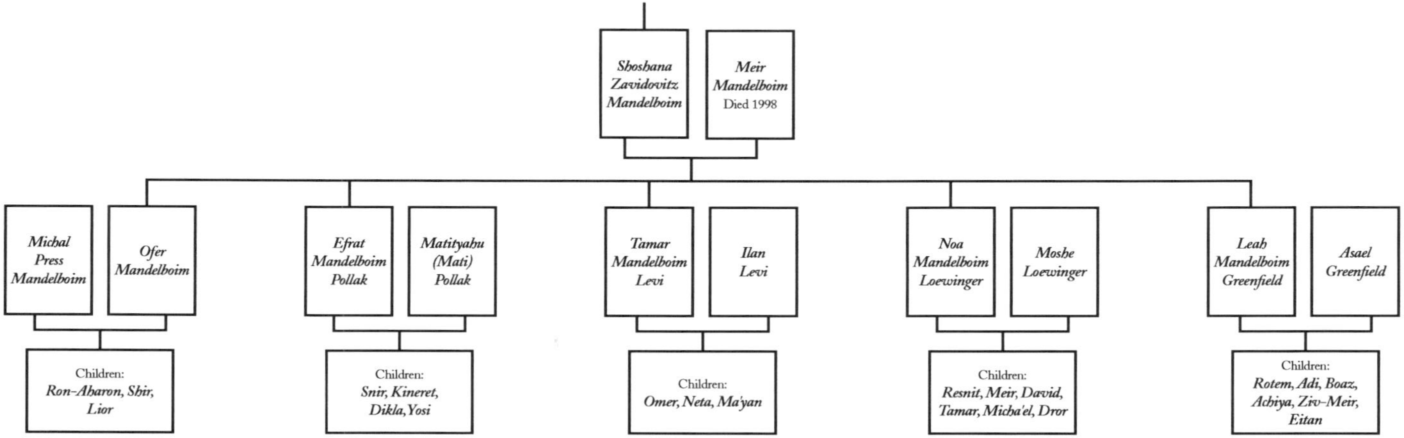

- Shoshana Zweidovitz Mandelboim — Meir Mandelboim (Died 1998)
  - Michal Press Mandelboim — Ofer Mandelboim
    - Children: Ron-Aharon, Shir, Lior
  - Efrat Mandelboim Pollak — Matityahu (Mati) Pollak
    - Children: Snir, Kinneret, Dikla, Yosi
  - Tamar Mandelboim Levi — Ilan Levi
    - Children: Omer, Neta, Ma'yan
  - Noa Mandelboim Loewinger — Moshe Loewinger
    - Children: Resnit, Meir, David, Tamar, Michael, Dror
  - Leah Mandelboim Greenfield — Asael Greenfield
    - Children: Rotem, Adi, Boaz, Achiya, Ziv-Meir, Eitan

Family of Freda's Father, Nosson Nuta Perelmuter

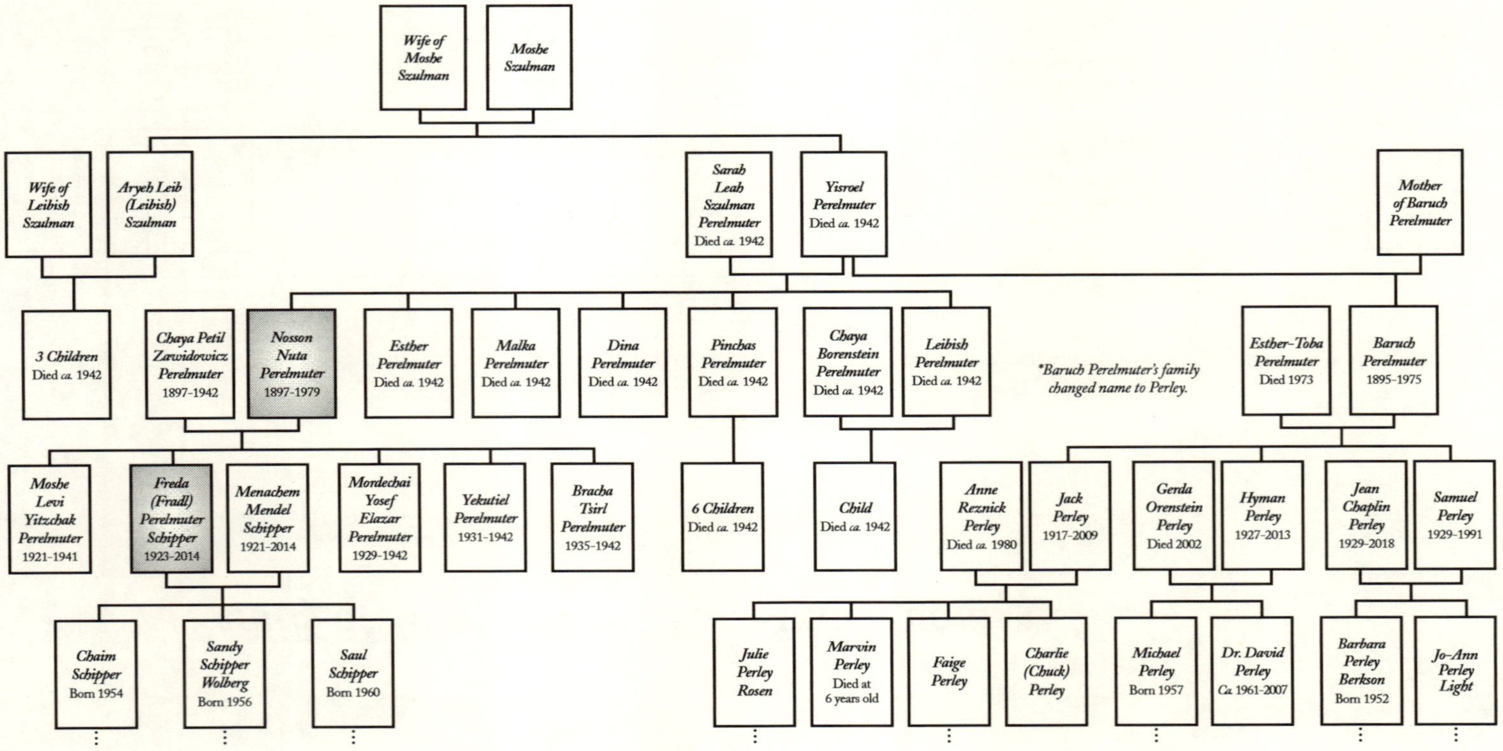

*Baruch Perelmuter's family changed name to Perley.

Family of Freda's Husband, Menachem Mendel Schipper

245

- Chaya Rachel Engelberg — Avraham Todros Engelberg
  - Sarah Engelberg Schipper (Died ca. 1940)
  - Chaim Schipper (Died ca. 1940)
  - *Other Siblings Continued Next Page*
  - Tzvi Hersh (Herman) Schipper 1911-1990 — Shaindel Szaffran Schipper 1925-1996
    - Chaim Schipper Born 1950 — Felicia Puchal Schipper Born 1950
      - Sina Schipper Nechushtan Born 1977 — Ido Nechushtan Born 1984
        - Yair Nechushtan Born 2007
        - Yaara Nechushtan Born 2007
        - Yabel Nechushtan Born 2012
  - Menachem Mendel Schipper 1921-2014 — Freda (Frradl) Perelmuter Schipper 1923-2014
    - Rachel Leah Rubinstein Schipper Born 1957 — Chaim (Hyman) Schipper Born 1954
      - Natan Yehoshua (Tani) Schipper Born 1996
      - Alter Dovid Schipper Born 1998
    - Sandy Schipper Wolberg Born 1956 — George Wolberg Born 1964
      - Jeffrey Wolberg Born 2002
    - Stephanie Kapusta Schipper Born 1962 — Saul Schipper Born 1960
      - Zoe Schipper Born 1995
      - Sarah Schipper Born 2001
      - Mayah Schipper Born 2001
      - Danielle Schipper Born 2005

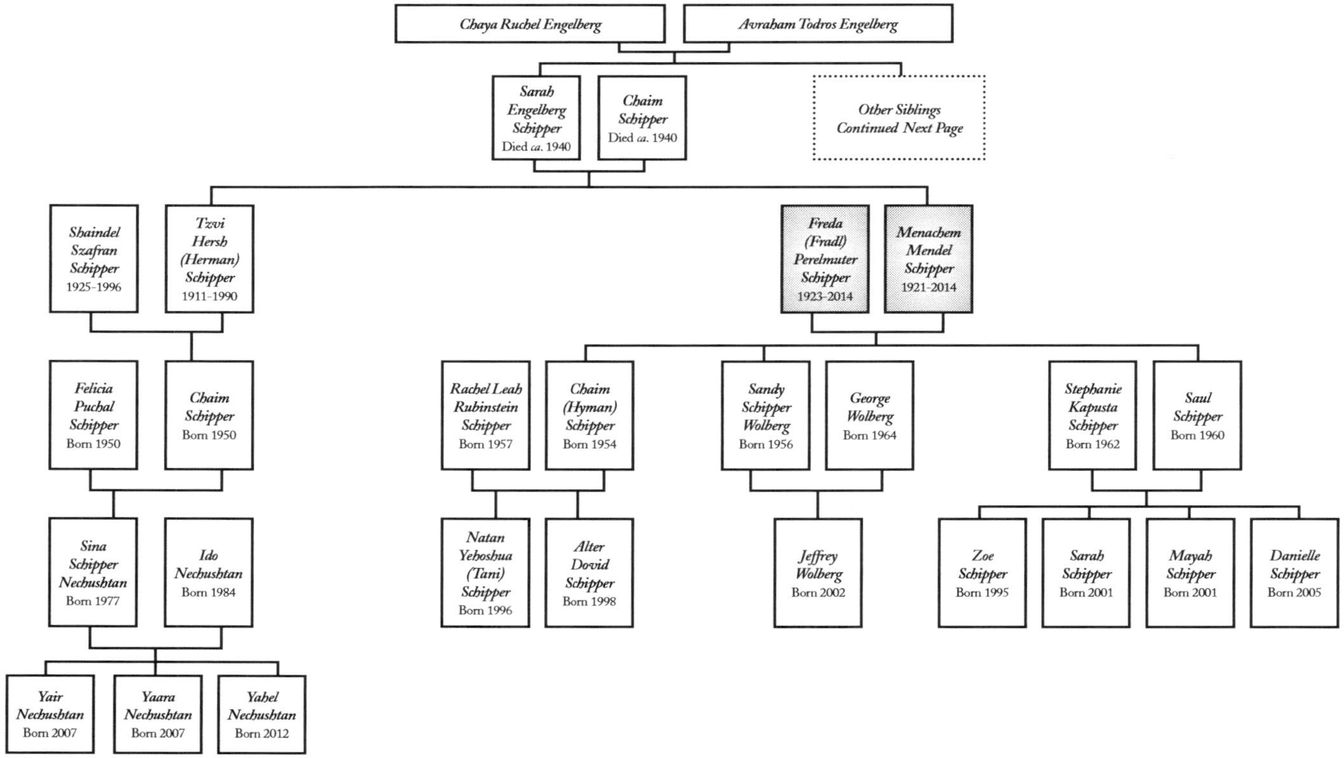

Family of Freda's Husband, Menachem Mendel Schipper (Continued)

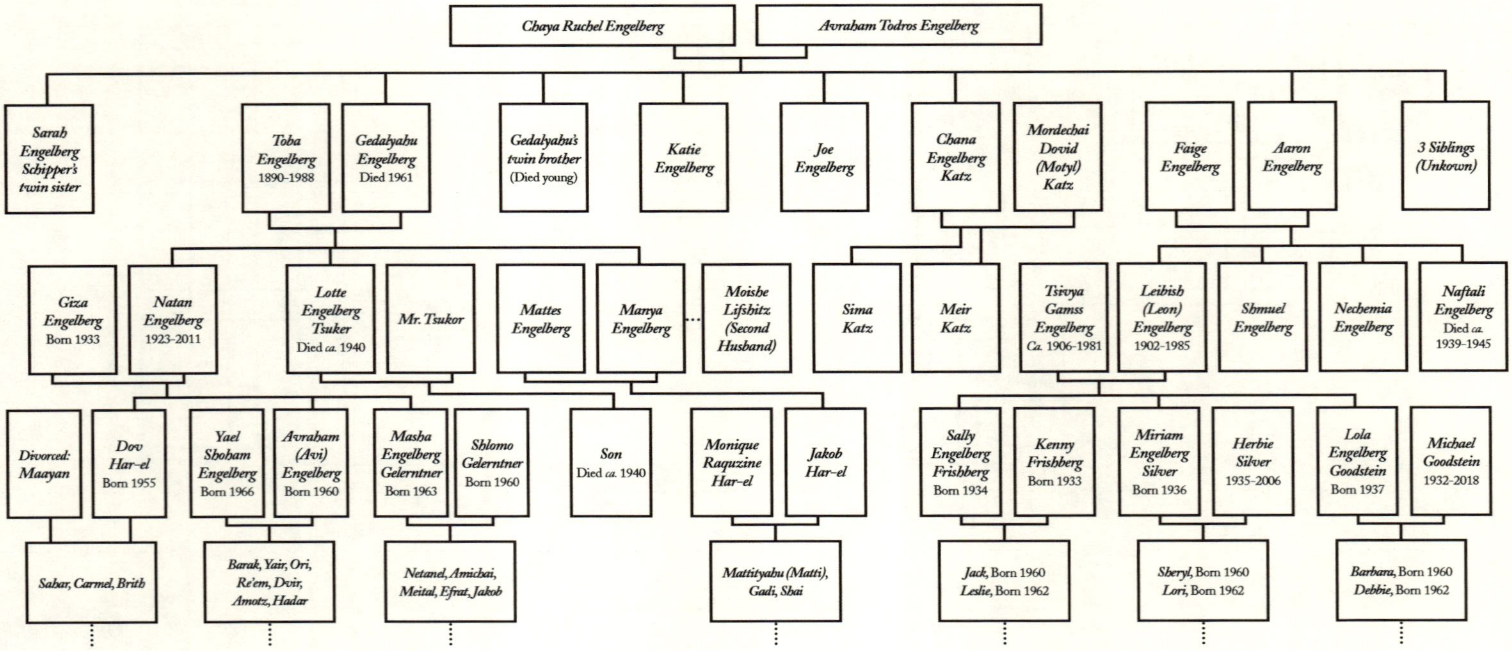

Family tree diagram with the following structure:

Parents: Chaya Ruchel Engelberg & Avraham Todros Engelberg

Siblings (with note: Sarah Engelberg, Schipper's twin sister; and Gedalyahu's twin brother, Died young):
- Toba Engelberg 1890-1988
- Gedalyahu Engelberg Died 1961
- Katie Engelberg
- Joe Engelberg
- Chana Engelberg Katz = Mordechai Dovid (Motyl) Katz
- Faige Engelberg
- Aaron Engelberg
- 3 Siblings (Unknown)

Children of Toba Engelberg:
- Giza Engelberg Born 1933
- Natan Engelberg 1923-2011

Children of Gedalyahu Engelberg:
- Lotte Engelberg Tsukor Died ca. 1940 = Mr. Tsukor

Children of Lotte Engelberg Tsukor:
- Matyo Engelberg = Moishe Lifshitz (Second Husband)
- Mattes Engelberg

Children of Chana Engelberg Katz & Mordechai Dovid Katz:
- Meir Katz
- Sima Katz

Children of Aaron Engelberg:
- Letibib (Leon) Engelberg 1902-1985 = Tsirya Gams Engelberg ca. 1906-1981
- Nechemia Engelberg
- Shmuel Engelberg
- Naftali Engelberg Died ca. 1939-1945

Children of Letibib (Leon) & Tsirya Engelberg:
- Sally Engelberg Frisberg Born 1934 = Kenny Frisberg Born 1933
- Miriam Engelberg Silver Born 1936 = Herbie Silver 1935-2006
- Lola Engelberg Goodstein Born 1937 = Mitzhael Goodstein 1932-2018

Descendants:
- Dvorrat: Maayan
- Dov Har-el Born 1955
- Yael Shoham Engelberg Born 1966
- Avraham (Avi) Engelberg Born 1960
- Masha Engelberg Gelertner Born 1963 = Shlomo Gelertner Born 1960
- Son Died ca. 1940
- Monique Raquzine Har-el
- Jakob Har-el
- Jack, Born 1960
- Leslie, Born 1962
- Sheryl, Born 1960
- Lori, Born 1962
- Barbara, Born 1960
- Debbie, Born 1962

Further descendants:
- Sahar, Carmel, Brith
- Barak, Yair, Ori, Re'em, Dvir, Amots, Hadar
- Natanel, Amichai, Meital, Efrat, Jakob
- Matityahu (Matti), Gadi, Shai

Note: Dov Engelberg and Jakob Engelberg changed their family name to Har-el

246

APPENDIX V

My Surviving Family Members

by
Freda Perelmuter Schipper

My father's half-brother, Baruch, his wife, Toba, and their young son, immigrated to Canada before the war.

My father's cousin Mendel Szulman and his family survived the war in the USSR, and eventually settled in Israel. He had three daughters and a son.

Yosef Chaim Zawidowicz, my first cousin, left for Israel before the war. He met Leah Shankman, originally from Ponevezh (Panevezys), Lithuania, in Israel and they married in 1939. They had one daughter whose name is Shoshana Mandelboim. Shoshana has five children (one son and four daughters) and many grandchildren and great-grandchildren. They all live in Israel.

Yosef's brother, Yehoshua Zawidowicz, fled from Poland to the Soviet Union before the German occupation and joined the labor regiment of the Soviet army (the Soviets did not let the Poles serve in the regular armed forces because they did not trust them). He met his wife, Rachel (Rosa), from one of the lands of the Soviet Union, in Asia and married her there. After the war they returned to Poland, then moved to Germany and finally made *Aliyah* (immigrated) to

Israel. They had three children but their eldest died about forty years ago. Their son and daughter live in Israel.

My first cousin Fradl (Chedva) Zawidowicz Zweig also went to Israel before the war. She has two daughters who live in Israel.

Fradl Zweig's brother, Yankel Zawidowicz, survived the war and went to the United States. He had two children, a son, Yosef, and a daughter, Libby.

My husband's brother, Hersh, married Shaindel Shafran, also a survivor and they had one son, Chaim Schipper. Chaim married Felicia, also a daughter of Holocaust survivors. They have one daughter, Sina, who is married to Ido Nechushtan. The Nechushtans have three children, two boys and a girl, Yair Yaakov, Yahel Moshe Tzvi, and Yaara Shaindel. They all live in Israel.

One of my husband's uncles, Gedalyahu Engelberg, (his mother's brother) and his wife, Toba, survived in the Soviet Union. They had two children, Natan and Manya. Manya married a cousin, Mattes Engelberg and they had a son they named Jakob. Natan married Giza and had three children, two sons and a daughter (Dov, Avraham and Masha). They each have large families and live in Israel.

Another one of my husband's first cousins, Leibish (Leon) Engelberg and his wife, Tsivya (Celia) Gamss, survived the war in Poland by hiding in an attic with their three young daughters, Sally, Miriam, and Lola. They, in turn, have two children each with children of their own. They live in the United States.

APPENDIX VI

Yizkor

by
Freda Perelmuter Schipper

DECEMBER 3, 1939 – My father's cousin, Moshe Szulman, was murdered on the death march from Chelm to Belzec. His father, Leibish Szulman, one of Bubbe Sarah Leah's brothers, died in his home when he heard that his son was killed with the 2,000 others on this death march. Leibish's wife and his two daughters also perished in the Holocaust.

JUNE 22, 1941 – Malke Zawidowicz Zucker, age 38, my mother's sister, and her six-year-old daughter, Fradale, were buried alive in Volodymyr.

SEPTEMBER 30, 1941 – *Erev Yom Kippur,* my brother, Moshe Levi Yitzchak Perelmuter, age 20, was shot and killed near the Volodymyr prison.

1941 – Mordechai Zawidowicz, my maternal uncle, was murdered in Lvov, Ukraine. His wife, Malke Zawidowicz, and one of their daughters, Surale, were taken away and perished in a death camp.

In August 1942, while in Starzeń, I received the encrypted postcard from their other daughter, Chanale (Hanka), who was in Lvov. This was the last time I heard from my young cousin.

1942 – Yekutiel Zawidowicz, my maternal uncle, and his wife, Paula Halpern Zawidowicz were murdered in the Warsaw ghetto. My maternal uncle, Fishel Zawidowicz and his wife and their daughter Fradl, were also murdered in 1942.

In 1942, my great-uncle, Rabbi Moshe Gelernter, my *bubbe* Ziesl's brother, was murdered in the cemetery in Volodymyr. His wife, two daughters and a son, Harav Heshel Gelernter, were killed and buried in a mass grave in Volodymyr, in the village of Piatydni.

MAY 16, 1942 – The Radziner Rebbe, Harav Shmuel Shloime Leiner, known as the Partisanner Rebbe for his directives to the Jews to take up arms and fight, was murdered in Volodymyr, 29 Iyar 5702, shortly after the slaughter of his wife and six children.

JUNE 10, 1942 – My mother, Chaya Petil Zawidowicz Perelmuter (age 49), my brothers Mordechai Yosef Elazar (age 13) and Yekutiel (age 11), and my little sister, Bracha Tsirel (age 7), were taken by train, together with all the Jews from Horodlo, from Miaczyn to die in the crematoria of Sobibor.

My mother's uncle, Rabbi Moshe Yehuda Leib Halevi Berman, and his entire family who remained in Poland, were in this deportation and perished in Sobibor.

SEPTEMBER 1, 1942 – Avner Zucker, my aunt Malke Zawidowicz's husband, and their son, Leibale, my aunt, Chana Zawidowicz Tennebaum, her husband, Moishe Tennenbaum, their three children, Leibel, Ziskind, and Fradl, and Pearl Biderman Zawidowicz were all murdered near Piatydni by a mobile killing squad.

NOVEMBER 13, 1942 – My *bubbe*, Ziesl Gelernter Zawidowicz, my aunt, Ruchel Boksenboim Zawidowicz, and a niece of Pearl Zawidowicz, whose name was Chaya Zisberg were all murdered in another *Aktion* near the Volodymyr prison.

Bubbe Ziesl's sister, Bina Gelernter Berger, her son, Henoch, and daughter, Chuma, Chuma's husband, Moshe Halpern, and their two daughters, Fradl and Eta, all perished in the Holocaust. They were from Hrubieshow.

1944 – My first cousins, Moshe and Yekutiel Zawidowicz, two sons of Pearl Biderman Zawidowicz, were murdered by the Pole who hid them, one month before the Soviets liberated Volodymyr.

Bracha Czesner Zawidowicz, a cousin's wife, perished in the Holocaust.

My father's parents, Sarah Leah (Szulman) and Yisroel Perelmuter – murdered.

My father's brother, Pinchas Perelmuter, his wife and 6 children, murdered in Krasnostav, Poland.

My father's other brother, Aryeh Leib Perelmuter, his wife, Chaya Borenstein Perelmuter and their young daughter were murdered in Izbica, Poland.

My father's three young sisters, Esther, Malke and Dina Perelmuter, perished in Chelm.

Most of my father's aunts, uncles, and cousins, perished in Sobibor.

My husband's parents, Sarah (Engelberg) and Chaim Schipper murdered in Kanczuga, Poland.

Sarah's sister, Faige Engelberg, and another sister, Chana Engelberg Katz, her husband, Mordechai Dovid (Motyl) Katz and their two children, Meir and Sima, all perished in Kanczuga, Poland.

Sarah's brother, Aaron Engelberg and his son, Naftali, were murdered in Kanczuga, Poland.

My husband's cousins, Lota (Engelberg) and Salek Zucker and their child, perished in Tarnow, Poland.

My husband's cousin, Chaya Schiffman and her family, including a son, Chaim, murdered.

These are the names I remember ...

Acknowledgments

Writing this memoir has been a true labor of love. I will always cherish the closeness I felt towards my mother as she meticulously recounted her life story during her final three months. Although my mother had eagerly shared her Holocaust memories with me, I never had a true understanding of the sequence in which they occurred. Speaking to her on a nightly basis as we worked on her memoir crystallized my admiration for her resilience, determination, and faith. Despite the sadness she had endured during the most barbaric period of human history, she never let that pain define her life. I will always treasure her, and I miss her dearly. Perhaps this book took me eight years to publish because I was reluctant to have this cathartic experience end.

I am infinitely indebted to my beloved father, Menachem Mendel Schipper, z"l. My father epitomized honesty, intelligence, grace, courage, compassion, and a strong work ethic. Unlike my mother, he was reticent to recount his wartime experiences, tending more to steer dinner conversations to the boundless blessings of present times and visions of a glorious Jewish future. More than the many communal acts of *chesed* (charitable acts) that punctuated my father's existence, it is the pleasure he distilled from every moment of family life that I will treasure most. In his quiet demeanor, he represented all that is good in this world. I am exceedingly grateful to my parents for the abundance of love they infused in our home.

I would like to thank Dr. Mitchell Bard for his discerning eye and writing expertise, which guided me through my countless revisions. An established author on Israel and the Holocaust, Dr. Bard is the Executive Director of the American-Israeli Cooperative Enterprise (AICE), and the director of the Jewish Virtual Library. He helped frame my mother's narrative within a precise historical context. Marcela Kogan Bard, writer, was instrumental in bringing to life some of my fondest and most profound memories of my mother and our relationship. This would not have been possible without her probing questions, fervor, and enduring patience.

Thank you to Azriella Jaffe, writer and editor, who kept telling me that I am an excellent writer, and when I did not believe her, she told me again, and again, and again.

I'd also like to thank Orah Ritholtz for her expertise in layout, formatting, typesetting and cover design. Her ever-patient demeanor proved invaluable as I worked through the many iterations of the family tree.

I'd like to extend my gratitude to my longtime friend and graphic designer, Faige Isler, for all her assistance with the photos and cover layout.

My heartfelt thanks to the ever-patient and gentle Yaakov Wasilewicz, who translated my mother's Polish notebooks, documents, and the letters my parents exchanged with each other when they first met. With his translation, Yaakov provided me with a window into the emotional intimacy and happiness my parents experienced during their courtship. I was tickled with excitement to have learned of their joy in finding each other and their hopes for starting a new life together.

Thanks to Janine Nathan for her helpful review of my manuscript. What a surprise it was to learn after we had become friends, that she is the granddaughter of my mother's DP camp friends, Ucia and Srulek Schwechter. The world is truly a small one!

A special thank you to my brothers, Chaim and Saul Schipper, for their continuous support and review of the manuscript. It was heartwarming for me to connect with my brothers over touching recollections of our mother and father. We consider ourselves blessed to have been the beneficiaries of our parents' unconditional love.

My sister-in-law, Ruchie Rubenstein Schipper (Chaim's wife), had an incredibly close and loving relationship with my mother. Having spent many *Shabbos* afternoons together intimately sharing their life stories, Ruchie became my mother's close confidante. As such, she provided insightful feedback. While this memoir touched upon many sad events, Chaim, Ruchie, and I reveled as we reminisced about all my mother's Yiddish idioms that spoke to her character and wit.

I owe a tremendous debt of gratitude to my wonderful, loving husband, George Wolberg. I could not have completed this book without his constant assistance, detailed comments, and enthusiastic support throughout all phases of this writing. He spent countless hours helping me edit the manuscript and served as an invaluable sounding board. I am truly blessed to have found my soulmate.

And finally, a big thank you to the light of my life – my son, Jeffrey, who has grown and matured alongside the writing of this book. His assistance in editing the manuscript and his praise of this book meant the world to me. Jeffrey's intelligence, drive, and determination remind me so much of my parents. I know they are watching from heaven, ever so proud of the young man he has become. May he always embody their virtues.

Made in the USA
Middletown, DE
28 November 2024